W9-ABR-453

Twayne's Filmmakers Series
Warren French, Editor

STEVEN SPIELBERG

STEVEN SPIELBERG

Donald R. Mott
Cheryl McAllister Saunders

TWAYNE PUBLISHERS • BOSTON
A Division of G.K. Hall & Co.

Steven Spielberg

Donald R. Mott
Cheryl McAllister Saunders

Copyright © 1986 by G. K. Hall & Co.
All Rights Reserved
Published by Twayne Publishers
A Division of G. K. Hall & Co.
70 Lincoln Street, Boston, Massachusetts 02111

Copyediting supervised by Lewis DeSimone
Book design and production by Marne B. Sultz
Typeset in 10 pt. Aster with Eras display type
by Compset, Inc., of Beverly, Massachusetts

Printed on permanent/durable acid-free paper
and bound in the United States of America

Library of Congress Cataloging in Publication Data

Mott, Donald R.
  Steven Spielberg.

  (Twayne's filmmakers series)
  Bibliography: p. 170
  Filmography: p. 177
  Includes index.
  1. Spielberg, Steven, 1947–   —Criticism and interpretation.   I.
Saunders, Cheryl McAllister.   II. Title.   III. Series.
PN1998.A3S6843   1986   791.43'0233'0924   86-220

ISBN 0-8057-9307-0 (Hardcover)
     0-8057-9311-9 (Paperback)

Contents

About the Authors

Donald R. Mott, associate professor of communication at Xavier University in New Orleans, is a native of New York City. He received his M.A. and M.F.A. in drama and communications (with a specialization in film and television) from the University of New Orleans and his Ph.D. from Louisiana State University. His publications include articles and reviews on film and broadcasting.

Cheryl McAllister Saunders is the former managing editor of the *Southern Quarterly* and holds B.A. and M.A. degrees in English from the University of Southern Mississippi. The author of articles and reviews on the arts, she has a special interest in women's studies and has begun work on a doctorate in English at Tulane University.

Editor's Foreword

This series of books premiered in 1977 with a review of the career of Francis Ford Coppola, then at the height of his glamorous reputation for the *Godfather* films, although bogged down in another ambitious project. *Apocalypse Now* finally reached the screen in 1979; but this costly and controversial film did not restore Coppola to the place in the filmmaking pantheon that had been taken over by two younger directors—one his protégé—with equally lofty aspirations, whose instincts seemed more closely attuned to contemporary audience preferences. The year this series began was an auspicious one in American movie history, for it was then that George Lucas's *Star Wars* and Steven Spielberg's *Close Encounters of the Third Kind* broke existing records to launch the renaissance of American cinema. At shopping-center theaters all over the country these "kid" pictures appealed to the romantic yearnings and frustrations of suburban teenagers.

Spielberg especially proved himself a master by establishing his first record with his second film made for theatrical distribution, the original *Jaws* (1975), the pinnacle of the "disaster films" that had kept movie houses open during the 1970s. These hair-raisers were becoming repetitive, however, and nothing that followed outclassed Spielberg's shark. The disaster films seemed ironically to be earning their generic title by following into oblivion the blockbuster "road show" musicals and exotic adventure tales of the 1960s. Theater owners were wondering whence salvation might come. Out of the skies it appeared, with *Star Wars* and *Close Encounters of the Third Kind*.

Both Lucas and Spielberg have continued their involvement with space travelers, but Lucas has left the direction of sequels to other hands, and they have not improved upon the record of the original spectacle. Spielberg, on the other hand, achieved his greatest triumph in 1982 by bringing the extra-terrestrial down to earth in *E.T.*, which marks so far both the zenith of his meteoric career and of Hollywood's quest for the ever bigger box office bonanza.

The future is mysterious. Spielberg's "prequel" to *Raiders of the Lost Ark* (1981), *Indiana Jones and the Temple of Doom* (1984), proved not so successful commercially or critically as the original and was seriously challenged as top grosser for the year by his sideline product *Gremlins*. In 1985 space operas began to falter at the box office. During the Christmas season the long-anticipated film version of Frank Herbert's *Dune*, *2010* (the sequel to the triumphant *2001*), and *Starman* (once considered an alternative to *E.T.*) failed to match the record-breaking receipts of the Spielberg/Lucas films. Even *E.T.* failed to repeat its earlier success when it was rereleased during the summer of 1985. The crowds were trooping instead to such black (in several senses of the word) comedies as *Ghost Busters* and *Beverly Hills Cop*. Has the Spielberg wave crested? Is his brightest future as executive producer developing the projects of others, like *Gremlins* and the much-praised *Back to the Future* (1985), or in new television ventures like "Amazing Stories"? Have distant planets lost their appeal as we enter a new age of urban street comedies? What will be the impact of mushrooming sales of videotapes on the future of film?

This book appears at as significant a point in Spielberg's career as the book about Coppola marked in his. Will Spielberg be able to move with changing tastes or will he be supplanted as pacesetter? Coppola's position in the film firmament has certainly declined since the *Godfather* days; but *The Cotton Club* proves that he is still an extraordinary artist with a vision that could be responsible for a memorable sequence of personal films. We need to recall that even Alfred Hitchcock, although he remained one of our most respected filmmakers, failed to maintain steadily the position that he won during the decade between 1935 and 1945 with his classic British films from *The Thirty-Nine Steps* to *The Lady Vanishes* and his first American films from *Rebecca* to *Spellbound*.

In retrospect it may prove that the first decade of this series has coincided with a distinctive chapter in the history of an industry increasingly ruled from Hollywood, even if its truly international products are now rarely made there. Whatever the future of this series may be, it will certainly have to make changes to keep up with an ever-changing medium in an ever-changing world.

W.F.

Preface

Steven Spielberg has been responsible for some of the most phenomenally successful films ever made. He combines a unique ability to identify with his audience with a creative use of technology and film history. Few directors have captured the popular imagination as well as this still youthful rhetorician of film.

Although Spielberg has been the subject of numerous fan-oriented publications, this is the first attempt at an in-depth study of his films. A retrospective, it includes brief biographical information, a discussion of early influences, and a look at Spielberg's first ten years as a feature film director.

The first two chapters provide biographical material, background on his early career as a television director, and a discussion of his first feature film, *The Sugarland Express* (1974). Chapters 3, 4, and 5 are each devoted to individual films— *Jaws, Close Encounters of the Third Kind,* and *1941.* His two collaborative efforts with friend and fellow filmmaker George Lucas—*Raiders of the Lost Ark* and *Indiana Jones and the Temple of Doom*—are treated in Chapter 6. Chapter 7 deals with the film most critics agree is Spielberg's finest directorial work—*E.T.: The Extra-Terrestrial.* Chapters 8 and 9 concentrate on film projects to which Spielberg has contributed his talents as producer-director—*Twilight Zone: The Movie*—and writer-producer—*Poltergeist*—as well as executive producer— *I Wanna Hold Your Hand, Used Cars, Gremlins, The Goonies,* and *Back to the Future.* Chapter 9 includes Spielberg's other projects, most notably his weekly series on NBC, "Amazing Stories," for which he has directed two episodes in the 1985–86 season; the release of two films he has produced for Christmas 1985 release, *The Money Pit* and *Young Sherlock Holmes;* and his film adaptation of Alice Walker's *The Color Purple,* considered a radical departure from his usual themes.

Chapters on individual films include background material on the production and planning stages, special effects (an important element in Spielberg's films), a critical analysis, and a look at contemporary reactions to each film.

As an exception to the format of this series, there are no illustrations of the films discussed here. Although illustrations are available, it was not possible to obtain the necessary permissions to reprint either from Mr. Spielberg's offices or from any of the major studios without direct permission from Steven Spielberg. The authors did not want to infringe in any way on Mr. Spielberg's rights and so could not print illustrations without proper authorization. We feel this should not detract from what is meant to be a serious analysis of the films, most of which are widely available to the viewing public. A list of currently available films with rental information is included in the Filmography.

Donald R. Mott
Cheryl McAllister Saunders

Acknowledgments

Many people deserve our gratitude and praise for their contributions to this project. We owe special thanks to Warren French for his tactful and helpful editing of the manuscript. His enthusiasm and knowledge of film made it a pleasure to work with him. Our thanks also go to Wayne and Mary Schuth and Peggy Whitman Prenshaw for their encouragement and support, as well as to Jimmy Howard for his invaluable research assistance.

On a personal level, we should acknowledge our friends and family for their patience, especially our son Thomas, who, once again, endured it all.

Chronology

1947   Steven Spielberg born 18 December in Cincinnati, Ohio, eldest child of Arnold and Leah Posner Spielberg.

1959   Turns out first 8-mm film with actors.

1960   Wins contest with forty-minute war film, *Escape to Nowhere.*

1963   Produces and directs 140-minute film, *Firelight.*

1964   *Firelight* premieres at a Phoenix, Arizona theater the night before Spielberg moves with his family to San Francisco, where father and mother later divorce.

1966   Begins work on a film called *Slipstream,* which is never completed.

1968   When knocking on studio doors fails to open them, produces and directs a short 35-mm film entitled *Amblin'.*

1969   Wins award at Atlanta Film Festival with *Amblin'.* When friend Chuck Silvers shows it to Sidney Sheinberg at Universal, Sheinberg offers Spielberg a seven-year contract that Spielberg signs. Leaves California State College, never earning his B.A. Begins work on "Night Gallery" pilot, directing one of three stories.

1970   *Amblin'* is distributed nationally, paired as a short with *Love Story.* Continues work at Universal on a variety of television series.

1971   Makes his first television movie, *Duel,* telecast by ABC on 13 November. Immediately begins his second television movie, *Something Evil,* for CBS.

1972   *Something Evil* telecast by CBS on 21 January. Almost a year later, he begins filming *Savage* for producers Richard Levinson and William Link.

1973   *Savage* airs on 31 March. Gains his first screenplay credit when *Ace Eli and Roger of the Skies* is released. *The Sugarland Express* story is developed by screenwriter friends Hal Barwood and Matt Robbins. The film is completed by September.

1974   *The Sugarland Express,* released by Universal Pictures, is praised by the critics but does very poorly at the box office. *Duel* is released in Europe as a feature, and Universal sends him there on a publicity tour. Producers Richard Zanuck and David Brown hire Spielberg to direct *Jaws* from Peter Benchley's bestselling novel of the same title. Filming begins in late spring and lasts until early fall. Work underway on *Close Encounters of the Third Kind.*

1975   *Jaws* is released by Universal Pictures during the summer and becomes the highest grossing film to that time, exceeding $100 million in its initial release. Begins preproduction work on *Close Encounters.*

1976   Begins production on *Close Encounters.* Special effects by Douglas Trumbull take more than a year to complete after shooting schedule with actors is completed.

1977   Spielberg and Lucas discuss making *Raiders of the Lost Ark* after the early summer of release of *Star Wars.* Columbia Pictures releases *Close Encounters of the Third Kind* in late fall.

1978   Acts as executive producer for *I Wanna Hold Your Hand.* Reshoots and reedits *Close Encounters* for the special edition. Begins work on *1941,* a comedy written by protégés Robert Zemeckis and Bob Gale.

1979   Universal releases the special edition of *Close Encounters of the Third Kind. 1941* is released by joint venture of Universal Studios and Columbia Pictures.

1980   Begins work on *Raiders of the Lost Ark* with George Lucas.

1981   *Raiders of the Lost Ark* released by Paramount Pictures. Begins work on *E.T.: The Extra-Terrestial.* Coauthors and produces *Poltergeist* with Tobe Hooper as director.

1982   *E.T.: The Extra-Terrestial* is released by Universal Pictures, and *Poltergeist* by Paramount Pictures that summer. Begins work on *Twilight Zone: The Movie* with each segment directed by a different director. Spielberg directs "Kick the Can" based upon an original "Twilight Zone" teleplay. Before the final segment is finished, a tragic accident on the set kills veteran actor Vic Morrow and two children. Spielberg, as producer, is cleared of any charges.

1983   Begins preproduction work in January for *Indiana Jones and the Temple of Doom.* Shooting begins in May in Sri Lanka (Ceylon). Becomes executive producer of *Gremlins,* directed by Joe Dante. Helps former film student Kevin Reynolds to make *Fandango* at Warner Brothers, but is not directly involved in the project.

1984   *Indiana Jones and the Temple of Doom* and *Gremlins* released by Paramount in May. Public outcry over excessive violence and horror in these films prompts the adoption of a new rating code, PG-13, that prohibits children under the age of thirteen from seeing such films without parental guidance.

1985   Produces two films for the summer trade—*The Goonies,* for which he wrote the story (released by Warner Brothers), and *Back to the Future,* directed by his friend Robert Zemeckis (released by Universal). Strikes a remarkable deal with NBC for a weekly series beginning in the fall titled "Amazing Stories," and directs two episodes for the first season. Begins filming Alice Walker's *The Color Purple* in June. Readies two films he produced—*The Money Pit* and *Young Sherlock Holmes*—for Christmas release, but *The Money Pit* is pulled from distribution. *The Color Purple* is released by Warner Brothers in December. Son, Max Samuel, is born. Marries actress Amy Irving.

1 / Steven Spielberg: The Director, the Man

Steven Spielberg gained worldwide popular and critical attention as the director of *Jaws*. An adaptation of Peter Benchley's novel, it has been described by movie critic Pauline Kael as a "cheerfully perverse scare movie," and by social critic I. C. Jarvie as a "very traditional shocker/disaster/monster movie," which was "brilliantly edited."[1] By breaking existing box office records, it earned its young director (he was twenty-seven when the film was released in 1975) a place in Hollywood lore.

The enormous success of *Jaws* coincides with a resurgence of interest in American filmmaking. In their 1979 study of the American film industry, *The Movie Brats*, Michael Pye and Linda Myles investigate the rise to power of a group of young filmmakers, including "wunderkind" Steven Spielberg. These talents—Francis Ford Coppola, George Lucas, Brian De Palma, Martin Scorsese and John Milius—combine an extensive knowledge of film and its history with an interest in modern technology. They have all created remarkable movie effects, but Spielberg and Lucas have had the most successful film careers to date.

Modern mythmakers, Spielberg and his friend Lucas set the style for filmmaking in the latter seventies and early eighties. Dressed in their familiar uniform of jeans, tee or rugby shirts, running shoes, baseball caps, and beards grown during production, they became models for their generation. Aspiring young directors donned the uniform and tried to emulate their heroes, who seemed to have saved movies from extinction by knowing what audiences wanted to see. Working apart and together (with George Lucas in the producer's role), they are responsible for the most financially successful films ever made. Admittedly, as noted by Pye and Myles, some of this financial success can be attributed to higher ticket prices and to more sophisticated publicity and marketing techniques.[2] As many a moviemaker has learned, however, publicity may bring people to the theater, but audiences decide a film's success or failure.

This popular success has caused many critics, including Seth Cagin and Philip Dray, to discount the importance of their work and label it "defiantly escapist."[3] Both Spielberg and Lucas have unabashedly admitted enjoying movies and wanting to re-create entertainment of the type they remembered from their childhoods. This philosophical agreement has enabled them to work well together, but Spielberg's directorial talents are at their best in the films that he has done without Lucas. His work shows unusual diversity and reflects his interest in technique and his ability to take risks within popular genres.

Spielberg is unique in that he is not a product of one of the nation's major film schools (Coppola's alma mater is the University of California–Los Angeles; Lucas attended the respected University of Southern California's film school, and Scorsese, New York University). Spielberg, whose high school grades were reportedly not high enough for the prestigious film schools (this, by the way, according to Lucas's biographer Dale Pollock, did not seem to prevent *his* admission to USC),[4] managed to create his own version of a film program at California State–Long Beach while majoring in English. This was only a foreshadowing of his enterprising spirit. During college, he went on to capture the attention of Sidney Sheinberg, then head of Universal Studio's television branch, with a short film, *Amblin'*. This film, which Spielberg describes as a "Pepsi commercial" because of its intentional commerciality, won awards in film competitions from Atlanta to Venice and landed its twenty-year-old creator a seven-year contract from Sheinberg.[5]

None of the other "movie brats" began his career in the

fast-paced, highly disciplined medium of television. Spielberg's television background is evident in the fast pacing he uses to hold an audience's attention, in his ability, when pushed, to work on very tight production schedules, and in his seeming lack of interest in films as "star vehicles" (television's actors are often subsumed by the exigencies of the medium).

His television experience puts Spielberg among the last of a generation of directors that includes Arthur Penn, Robert Altman, and William Friedkin. Jerzy Toeplitz refers to this group as "television generation" directors because they worked in television before films and were associated primarily with youth films.[6] In the sixties, so-called youth films usually made a political or antiestablishment statement, but by the seventies, Hollywood was turning to more escapist treatments. Spielberg would have to please audiences who were ready to leave Viet Nam and Watergate behind. The times were right for a young filmmaker with technical expertise who remembered with fondness the escapist entertainment of a fifties childhood.

Another quality that makes Spielberg unique among his peers is his seeming ability to work within the Hollywood "system," defined as the bureaucratic studio-production-distribution companies whose main consideration is "the bottom line," that is, "profit margins." Colleagues Coppola and Lucas broke early with the studios, setting up their own production companies, but Spielberg often works within the studio system and refers to himself as an "independent moviemaker working within the Hollywood establishment."[7]

Spielberg has had successful collaborations with most of the major film studios, including his home base, Universal (*The Sugarland Express*, 1974; *Jaws*, 1975; and *E.T.: The Extra-Terrestrial*, 1982), Columbia (*Close Encounters of the Third Kind*, 1977; and *1941*, 1979), Paramount (*Raiders of the Lost Ark*, 1981, and *Indiana Jones and the Temple of Doom*, 1984—in conjunction with Lucasfilm), and Metro-Goldwyn-Mayer (*Poltergeist*, 1982). His apprenticeship in television obviously served him, Universal, and his mentor, Sidney Sheinberg, well in the industry. In a 1982 listing of the top fifteen money-making films of all time, Spielberg had directed four—*Jaws*, *Close Encounters*, *Raiders of the Lost Ark*, and *E.T.*

Duel (1973), a made-for-television film, brought Spielberg recognition as a young director of unusual ability. Well received when it appeared on ABC television, it also attracted unusual attention abroad, winning a number of prestigious film awards and earning Spielberg notice from the *Cahiers du Cinéma* group in France.[8] Although he made two other full-length television films (*Savage* and *Something Evil*), *Duel* stands out. An unusual story by Richard Matheson, it features an eighteen-wheeler truck as the antagonist and Dennis Weaver as the harried victim; in Spielberg's hands *Duel* became a minor work of art.

This success won him the time to pursue a career in feature filmmaking; his first project, *The Sugarland Express*, appeared in 1974. Starring Goldie Hawn, it was not an entirely auspicious beginning, but it earned Spielberg generally good notices from critics. Pauline Kael, in particular, notes Spielberg's remarkable "sense of composition and movement" and compares him to Howard Hawks. She asserts, "in terms of the pleasure that technical assurance gives an audience, this film is one of the most phenomenal debut films in the history of movies."[9]

When *Jaws* was released in 1975, Kael was obviously less surprised than others by its phenomenal success. She has called Spielberg "a magician in the age of movies" (in an essay written after the 1977 release of *Close Encounters of the Third Kind*) and has written a number of perceptive essays that analyze Spielberg's unique strengths as well as his weaknesses.

His next project, for which he also wrote the screenplay, was *Close Encounters of the Third Kind*, a science fiction film. Here a distinct personal style emerged. Also well received by critics and the public, the film was a complete departure from his previous ones. It featured magnificent effects by Douglas

Trumbull, who had done the effects in *2001: A Space Odyssey*, but it also had a sweetness and warmth missing in the previous films. It served to break the image of a "shark and truck" director that he feared acquiring (*Sugarland*, incidentally, features beautifully orchestrated car-chase scenes).

1941 (1979) reflects another change of pace. A World War II comedy featuring a cast of literally hundreds (nearly every Hollywood actor—young and old—seems to appear) and complicated miniature sets, it fails for excess and overworked material. The script, written by Bob Gale and Robert Zemeckis (for whom Spielberg served as producer on *Used Cars* and *I Wanna Hold Your Hand*)), has too many plot lines and its humor, an otherwise laudatory television interviewer remarked, is "sophomoric." Although neither a commercial nor a critical success, the film is, as Jean-Pierre Coursodon and Pierre Sâuvage note, a highly original "*directorial* experiment, in which the crudeness of the gags is constantly contrasted with the dreamlike atmosphere generated by Spielberg's amazingly complex and inventive staging."[11] The film served to stretch the comic talents apparent in Spielberg's earlier work.

After the criticism for self-indulgence that Spielberg encountered after the release of *1941*, he was ready to show his more disciplined side when his budget-conscious friend George Lucas hired him to direct *Raiders of the Lost Ark*. The huge popular success of this film, intended as a revival of the old Saturday afternoon serials of the 1930s and 1940s, put Spielberg back on firm footing in Hollywood's bookkeeping departments, and he was able to begin two films—*Poltergeist* and *E.T.: The Extra-Terrestrial*—which, during production, he referred to in interviews as "A Boy's Life."[12]

Both released in 1982, these films were about Spielberg's "nightmares" and "good dreams," respectively. Since he could not direct (by union rules) both films simultaneously, officially he served as line producer for *Poltergeist*, which was directed by Tobe Hooper; nevertheless, Spielberg was involved in all stages of production, including the screenplay, which he coauthored from his own story. He served as director for *E.T.: The Extra-Terrestrial* and received a third Academy Award nomination (his films have won numerous Academy Awards, but he has never won in the coveted "best director" category). This film was his biggest success yet. A warm family film (interestingly enough, it was banned in Denmark for being too intense for youngsters under eleven), written by Melissa Mathison, it is reminiscent of Walt Disney's *Old Yeller* but features an unlikely best friend for a boy— a lovable, misplaced visitor from outer space.

Spielberg's 1983 release was *Twilight Zone: The Movie*, his attempt in collaboration with three other film directors— John Landis, Joe Dante, and George Miller—to recreate and pay homage to Rod Serling's unusually creative 1950s and early 1960s television series "The Twilight Zone." Spielberg directed one of the film's four segments, a reinterpretation of an original "Twilight Zone" episode, "Kick the Can." It featured his recognizable diffuse back-lighting technique. He also served as executive producer for the project, which was struck by tragedy when actor Vic Morrow and two small children were killed in a helicopter accident during the filming of John Landis's segment. The incident inspired a wave of safety reform throughout the Hollywood guilds. (Ironically, the tragedy occurred on the heels of two movies about stunt men whose maniacal directors insist on bigger, better, and more dangerous stunts—*The Stunt Man* [1980] starring Peter O'Toole and *Hooper* [1978] with Burt Reynolds.) It is not clear if the indifferent reception by audiences was the result of the tragedy, which was played up in the news media for weeks, or stemmed from the fact that younger audiences (which comprise much of the movie-going public) were unfamiliar with the original "Twilight Zone" series. Many critics and Spielberg fans said that they wanted "more from him" in his segment; by far, the most exciting and well-received part was directed by George Miller, who reworked an original "Twilight Zone" teleplay by Richard Matheson.

After this setback, the success of *Raiders of the Lost Ark* encouraged Spielberg to make good on his promise to Lucas to direct the sequel (or "prequel" as it was billed), *Indiana Jones and the Temple of Doom*, which appeared in May 1984. It was followed within weeks by *Gremlins*, a Steven Spielberg production directed by Joe Dante (who had directed a segment of *Twilight Zone*). *Temple of Doom* is most notable for its intense action, including excessive violence that Spielberg publicly acknowledged as too "intense" for young children. *Gremlins* also contains violent scenes, such as the mother liquidating a gremlin in her Mix-Master, and it, too, was deemed inappropriate for young children. Attacks on these films by critics, the media, and the public led to a new rating code, PG-13, which prohibits children under the age of thirteen from seeing such films without parental guidance. Spielberg, however, redeemed himself to his fans with the rerelease of *E.T.* in 1985. This year also marked a major change for director Spielberg with the release of his first film with an adult theme, an adaptation of Alice Walker's *The Color Purple*. Yet he kept active in the youth market, producing *The Goonies, Back to the Future, The Money Pit*, and *Young Sherlock Holmes*.

BACKGROUND

Steven Spielberg was no stranger to Hollywood studios when he went to work for Universal in 1970. As a teenager, he had spent many hours on the studio lots watching other directors, including Alfred Hitchcock. The fact that he had not been invited had not deterred young Spielberg, who claims he just arrived neatly dressed, carrying a briefcase. By looking the guard at the gate straight in the eye, he bluffed his way onto the lots. He admits being thrown off a number of sets, including those for Hitchcock's *Torn Curtain* (as a teenager) and *Family Plot* (after he had made *Jaws*).[13]

His parentage bears a striking resemblance to Orson

Welles's. Both his mother and Welles's were musical and both fathers were oriented toward science and engineering. Unlike Welles, who was an only child, Spielberg has three younger sisters, one of whom, Annie, has followed her brother into filmmaking.[14] Being the only son in "a house with three screaming younger sisters and a mother who played concert piano with seven other women," Spielberg feels he "was raised in a world of women."[15] His father also had an influence, however, introducing Spielberg to the world of science. He has remarked often on his father's interest in astronomy and of their trips to gaze at the stars.

Spielberg claims as a youngster to have been the family moviemaker, recording the usual special events, but also making Hollywood-style movies with his sisters and neighborhood children serving as casts.[16] One of these films, shown in a televised interview on ABC's "20/20," does exhibit, as noted by broadcast journalist Steve Fox, "an early intuitive knowledge of filmmaking."[17] The segment shows a youngster dressed in a leather jacket and helmet in a plane that appears, by its precarious angle and movement, to be crashing.

His mother, Leah Posner Spielberg, and father, Arnold Spielberg, seem to have been remarkably supportive of what must have been a rather expensive and harrowing childhood hobby. (Later, he showed his entrepreneurial talents by using a tree-painting business to help finance his film efforts).[18] In the "20/20" interview, Spielberg's mother (now Leah Adler) tells with a delightfully rueful smile of never being able to finish decorating her home. She remembers, "I lived in a beautiful house and I got as far as the carpeting, drapes and a Steinway and then he took over, and my house from the time I can remember it was a studio."[19]

In another interview, she recalls thinking her son—now often referred to as a "young genius"—more than a little "disingenuous," particularly when, as a little boy, he delighted in scaring his sisters with horror stories. She tells of one occasion when she and his father returned home from an evening out to find Steven in full-face monster makeup, consisting of wet "green toilet paper."[20]

After Steven's birth in Cincinnati in 1947, the family moved East to New Jersey and then West to Arizona and California. The moves were made to allow Arnold Spielberg to advance in his profession as an electrical engineer and computer expert.[21] Spielberg's adolescence was spent in Phoenix, where he attended high school. He continued to make films, financed partially by his father and by his tree-painting business, and won local fame with a feature-length film, *Firelight*. This film has been described as "a two-and-one-half-hour 8-mm epic about a team of scientists investigating mysterious lights in the night sky."[22] The film premiered at a local movie theater just before the family moved to California. His parents divorced after this move and Steven became the male head of the family at sixteen.

Spielberg had, by all accounts, a relatively normal, happy childhood, sharing experiences of the baby-boom generation—the first to be reared with television. He has often commented on the care his parents took to control his media viewing; to insure that he did not spend too much time in front of the idiot box, or view the wrong programs, they draped a blanket over the set.[23] Walt Disney films were an important part of his world, as for most of the children of his generation, for they were considered "family entertainment." He was sensitive enough to point out to his parents that much of what they considered to be wholesome, good, clean storytelling, also had its moments of terror for a child. (These films were made in a day before Bruno Bettelheim wrote his apologia for fairy tales, *The Uses of Enchantment*.) Spielberg recalls being frightened by such films as *Snow White* and *Fantasia* and telling his bewildered parents he was afraid after seeing *Bambi* because "the fire killed the family."[24]

This sheltered, thoroughly middle-class, childhood seems to have influenced much of Spielberg's life and work. Even *Jaws*, which Jarvie notes is "gory in the modern style," does not depend on gore to sell tickets, as do many of the films in the genre, but instead on Hitchcockian suspense, storytelling, and action. From this early film to his 1982 film, *E.T.: The Extra-Terrestrial* (which stars an alien that he conceived as an imaginary friend when he was "very lonely" at a foreign location on another film project),[25] the hallmark of Spielberg's best work has been a slightly mischievous and comic, but good-natured view of the world and humanity. Pauline Kael may have been the first critic to note this quality. In her comments for the *New Yorker* on *Close Encounters of the Third Kind* she says, "Spielberg may be the only director with technical virtuosity ever to make a transcendently sweet movie." The film "is so generous in its feelings that it makes one feel maternal and protective."[26] This is not to say that Spielberg's work is all sweetness and light—many of his films to date are in the horror or suspense genre and contain material of which nightmares are made—but the majority of his films (particularly the early ones) leave the audience feeling that the "average" man or woman has survived against seemingly insurmountable odds.

This interest in ordinary, everyday people who face situations much larger than they is a subject Spielberg has commented upon often. He claims a major theme of his films (at least before *E.T.*) has been of "people pursued by large forces."[27] This could hark back to his own childhood and his less than athletic size (he appears from photographs to have been a thin child and possibly small for his age). He seems to have early developed a sense of humor that enabled him to cope. A story he recounted to interviewer Michael Sragow describes his "school days of being a wimp in a world of jocks." He claims,

> The height of my wimpery came when we had to run a mile for a grade in elementary school. The whole class of fifty finished, except for two people left on the track—me and a mentally retarded boy. Of course, *he* ran awkwardly, but I was just never able to run. I was maybe forty yards ahead of him, and

I was only 100 yards away from the finish line. The whole class turned and began rooting for the young retarded boy—cheering him on, saying, "C'mon, c'mon, beat Spielberg! Run, run!" It was like he came to life for the first time, and he began to pour it on but still not fast enough to beat me. And I remember thinking, "Okay, now how am I gonna fall and make it look like I really fell?" And I remember actually stepping on my toe and going face hard into the red clay of the track and actually scraping my nose. Everybody cheered when I fell, and then they began to really scream for this guy: "C'mon, John, c'mon, run, run!" I got up just as John came up behind me, and I began running as if to beat him but not really to win, running to let *him* win. We were nose to nose, and suddenly I laid back a step, then a half-step. Suddenly he was ahead, then he was a chest ahead, then a length, and then he crossed the finish line ahead of me. Everybody grabbed this guy, and they threw him up on their shoulders and carried him into the locker room, into the showers, and I stood there on the track field and cried my eyes out for five minutes. I'd never felt better and I'd never felt worse in my entire life.[28]

His affinity for childhood and children and his ability to touch "the child in all of us" is remarked upon so often by critics and reviewers that it has become a cliché (Walt Disney used to have a monopoly here), but his films do show a good-humored sympathy for the "little person" in all humans. His storytelling ability and a self-deprecating humor suggest Charlie Chaplin. Julian Smith says, "Of all contemporary filmmakers, only Steven Spielberg seems to have the staying power to develop into a creator of comic adventures and fantasies about little men and women and children who fight and win on their own terms against bullying monsters and bureaucracies—against inexplicably maniacal trucks and sharks, against agencies both governmental and supernatural that seek to take away our lives, our chidren, or our dreams."[29]

His suburban childhood has been translated into the autobiographical fantasies of *Poltergeist*, *E.T.*, and *Close Encounters*, films that capture American life-styles and experiences.

His mother comments "You are viewing our family at the dinner table when you see *E.T.*"[30] Pye and Myles note the "almost archeological, attention to suburban detail" in *Close Encounters.*[31] In the first thirty minutes of *Poltergeist,* Spielberg firmly establishes his characters in suburban family life. It raises what he has referred to as a "ghost story" beyond the modern horror genre. The film also has the first really strong women's roles in any of his film work—the suburbanite mother, played by JoBeth Williams, and a parapsychologist, played by Beatrice Straight.

The young boy in the film is possibly the most autobiographical of all his characters. There is even some physical resemblance between its young star, Oliver Robins, and Spielberg as a child. *Poltergeist* is about Spielberg's "fears—of a clown doll, of a closet, of what was under my bed, of the tree in New Jersey that . . . moved whenever there was a wind storm."[32] It seems that in his most successful film work, Spielberg has followed the old adage "write what you know."

Influences from his childhood abound. Pye and Myles note his use of elements derived from Disney's animated features and Chuck Jones's Road Runner cartoons. Another important influence appears to be what Jarvie calls the "spectacle movies" of the fifties. These lavish productions featured advanced technical "gimmicks" such as "Cinerama, stereoscopic sound, CinemaScope, VistaVision, Todd-A.O., Super PanaVision, etc."[33] Spielberg and his parents saw movies like *The Greatest Show on Earth* (1954), which made an important impression on him. "My father said: 'It's going to be bigger than you, but that's all right. The people in it are going to be up on a screen and they can't get out at you.' But there they were up on that screen *and they were getting out at me.* I guess ever since then I've wanted to try to involve the audience as much as I can, so they no longer think they're sitting in an audience."[34] These spectacles influenced his lavish filmic style, which includes careful attention to lighting and cinematography (a field in which he has contributed articles to professional technical journals),[35] elaborate special effects executed as realistically as possible, musical scores that are an important emotional element, and often epic story lines. His cinematic style and his ability to be his own audience have created films that fulfill the needs of television-generation audiences for constant action but also have an honesty, a humanity, which is unique among American filmmakers since Frank Capra.

STYLE AND TECHNIQUE

A televised interview on ABC's newsmagazine "20/20" features Spielberg in a homey scene preparing avocados for a salad. Suddenly, what would have been a bland domestic scene is transformed into a moment of fantasy horror, Spielberg, stepping out of his role of interviewee and into his obviously more natural one of film director, takes over and instructs the camera crew to zoom in on his hand and to "hold the frame." "20/20"'s camera captures a huge butcher knife which appears to loom ominously over an imagined victim.[36]

This episode demonstrates perfectly Steven Spielberg's affinity with the camera and cinematic illusion. In an early *Newsweek* interview he observes, "making movies is an illusion, a technical illusion that people fall for"; his "job is to take that technique and hide it so well that never once are you taken out of your chair and reminded of where you are."[37] His technical expertise and ability to "see" as the lens "sees" have been widely admired and have earned him the respect of Hollywood's most exacting artists and technicians. He describes his cinematic style as "fast-paced, energetic, and filled with a lot of imagery and visuals."[38] He is noted, in particular, for the extensive storyboarding he does in preproduction. (Interestingly, he claims to have used this technique less than usual in his most admired film to date, *E.T.: The Extra-Terrestrial*).[39] Storyboarding entails breaking the final shooting script down into detailed pictures that represent the "ideal frame" (or frames) of a particular scene. Camera angles, direction, and camera and/or actor movements within a shot are specified. The visual construction of the script in this picture-book form (usually covering several walls in Spielberg's production office) means it can be easily honed and edited even before the cameras roll. Although such techniques have been criticized (as they were by Rosenbaum) for rendering a film "mechanical-looking"—they often stifle spontaneity and experimentation—the process assists the filmmaker in preventing delays in the shooting schedule, especially of scenes shot on location.

Early 8-mm films show Spielberg's storytelling abilities and an awareness of cinematic techniques such as montage and continuity. But, it was in his early television work that Spielberg searched for a unique personal style. There is an obvious attempt to emulate the European "art films" of the French New Wave of the fifties and sixties, typical of a late-sixties "film student." Allan Arkush notes, in his article in *Film Comment*, "I remember Film School," "in winter of 1969 I was a junior at N.Y.U. film school. . . . The cinema was not fun, it was art . . . and my pantheon consisted of Bergman, Antonioni, Resnais, Kurosawa and, most of all, Godard."[40] Spielberg seems to have developed a similar pantheon. The European influence is particularly obvious in his first undertaking at Universal, a segment of "Night Gallery," in which he directed Joan Crawford and Barry Sullivan. The episode contains numerous reflection and glass shots that symbolically reinforce the plot in which a rich, influential, but blind, woman tries to buy the only thing she doesn't possess—the ability to see. The reflection/mirror motif is used fairly extensively in *Duel*, more subtly in *The Sugarland Express*, and hardly at all in *Jaws*.

In searching for a comfortable but unique visual style, Spielberg eventually settled on a lighting effect that is heavily backlit and slightly diffused, which lowers the overall contrast and mutes the intense hues of color emulsion. Through this technique the semblance of natural lighting is achieved, but without the harshness usually obtained when film is shot under natural lighting conditions. The effect is slightly harrowing, almost surrealistic and visually off-key. The use of extensive backlighting and Spielberg's knowledge of montage hark back to early American cinema techniques from the silent era, recognized by Russian film scholar Lev Kuleshov in his study *The Art of Cinema*.[41] Spielberg's ability to use montage was probably developed during his early television years. Toeplitz feels that "characteristically the directors who have come to film from television, regard montage as a much more important part of their skills than did the film-makers of the thirties and forties. . . . They seem closer to the traditions of the silent screen."[42]

Although Spielberg prefers to work with fixed focal lenses (such as early filmmakers were forced to use) he occasionally uses the zoom lens technique, and sometimes in conjunction with the dolly shot. The effect of combining the zoom-out with a dolly-in produces visual anxiety, a sense of helplessness and isolation. By dollying the camera into the subject while the lens zooms out to a wide angle, the subject or object remains in the same position and retains the same size within the frame, but the background literally "explodes" outward from behind the subject. The reverse effect (a zoom-in with a dolly-out) visually "slides" the background toward the subject while retaining the subject's relative size within the frame. The effect creates the initial appearance of an exaggerated perspective of the background that is brought into proper alignment with the subject. Spielberg used the latter technique as early as the "Night Gallery" episode when Barry Sullivan, playing Joan Crawford's physician, enters her apartment. The camera, peering through a pear-shaped cut glass crystal hanging from a hallway chandelier, inverts Sullivan's image. As he walks into the room and toward the camera, the camera booms down, zooms in and dollies out, bringing Sullivan and the room into proper perspective, thus orienting the audience to the action.

Spielberg further developed and refined these dolly-zoom

techniques in *Duel* and *The Sugarland Express* (for the chase sequences), in *Jaws* (when Chief Brody witnesses the death of a young swimmer while he sits nervously on the beach), and in *Poltergeist* (when the young suburban mother attempts to race down a hallway to rescue her children).

The marriage of film history with technology, typical in Spielberg's peer group, has been termed "cine-literacy" by Pye and Myles (the concept is attributed to Myles), but Spielberg's work exhibits more technical virtuosity than the others. He is a great admirer of the old Hollywood masters, such as John Ford and Frank Capra; his films often contain embedded visual or aural references to them. Spielberg's films are slightly old-fashioned in plot, but are technically advanced, featuring state-of-the-art special effects from such noted masters as Bob Mattey (the former special effects wiz for Walt Disney designed the mechanical sharks for *Jaws*), Douglas Trumbull (*2001: A Space Odyssey*), and the Industrial Light and Magic Ltd., an offshoot of Lucasfilm.

2 / From Television to Feature Films

Spielberg made his debut as a television director with a segment of "Night Gallery," produced by Universal Television. The episode stars Joan Crawford as a wealthy but blind woman who makes her wish for sight come true by blackmailing a famous eye surgeon, played by Barry Sullivan, into performing an experimental operation. The surgeon is reluctant about the surgery because the results are only temporary. The premise of the show is that the woman will do anything for even a few hours of sight. After the operation, when Crawford removes the bandages at the appointed time (at night, when she is alone), an electrical blackout makes it appear that the operation was a failure. The darkness she was used to is still around her, and her temporary eyesight fails before the lights come back on. This type of plot twist is typical of the "Night Gallery" series.

Although Crawford and Sullivan were famous actors, by all accounts, Spielberg, only twenty-two, was undaunted by his stars' reputations and experience. The two turn in their usual polished performances, both very much in command of rather limited roles, which allowed Spielberg to concentrate on other aspects—an excellent way for an inexperienced director to start his career. It is not the acting that makes the episode notable, but the highly stylized camera techniques, particularly the dolly-zoom shot noted earlier, and Spielberg's symbolic use of light imagery. The symbolism, at times heavy-handed, is remarkable because such sophisticated techniques are seldom used in television. The segment shows the influences of new wave filmmakers on Spielberg's early work.

Spielberg next directed episodes of "The Psychiatrist," "Marcus Welby, M.D.," "The Name of the Game," and "Columbo" for Universal Television. Spielberg considers two episodes of "The Psychiatrist" as his best television work: "Jerry Friedman was the producer. . . . I was just a young person, whom he liked at the time, and to whom he said, 'Here, do two *Psychiatrists* for me.'"[1] One show was about death, the other about a six-year-old boy lost in a world of fantasy and comic books. Spielberg felt the episode about the dying golf pro was his best, since he was able to incorporate his own ideas into the story. It involved two friends who could not face another friend's death. To provide a moving climax Spielberg created a scene where the friends present the dying golfer with a shoe box containing the eighteenth hole from the golf course. "He tore the grass out of the hole and he squeezed the dirt all over himself and he thanked them for bringing this gift, the greatest gift he ever received. It was just a very moving moment that came out of being loose with an idea."[2] The other series, which included individual episodes longer than ninety minutes, such as "Name of the Game" and "Columbo," prepared Spielberg for the rigors of feature-length productions. In these longer teleplays Spielberg was able to develop the story and make his characters come to life.

Spielberg found working on "Columbo" "fun because the series was an experience in helping, but mostly watching, Peter Falk find this terrific character."[3] Two "Columbo" television movies had been shot before Spielberg did the first episode of the series, but Falk was still exploring his offbeat detective character for "Columbo-isms."

After his series work, Spielberg made three television movies—*Something Evil* (1970), *Duel* (1971), and *Savage* (1973). *Something Evil* was a project Spielberg "wanted to do," but he apparently resented directing *Savage*: "[It] was an assignment bordering on *force majeur*. [*Savage*] was the first and last time the studio ordered me to do something."[4] Of the three, *Duel* stands out as the finest example of Spielberg's unusual abilities as a television director.

<u>DUEL</u>

An adaptation of a short story by Richard Matheson, who also wrote the screenplay, *Duel* provided Spielberg a perfect showcase for his talents. It is an unusually well directed television movie (later released with additional scenes as a feature-length film in 1973) about a man on a routine business trip who is terrorized by an eighteen-wheeler. Through the use of unusual wide-angle shots and split-second choreography in the editing, the truck becomes a believable, ominous terror. The truck driver is never seen—except for his hands and boots.

The unusual story begins when David Mann (Dennis Weaver) leaves on a typical morning for an out-of-town business meeting. The story (in the feature-length version) opens from the car's point-of-view; David is seen only later when the car is already on the highway. The audience first gets a headlight's view as the car backs out of the driveway, drives through town, through a tunnel, and then onto the highway. Then we see David and the car itself. They both express simple lines—David neatly dressed in shirt, tie, and khaki pants with his seatbelt firmly buckled, and the vehicle, a typically plain, nondescript company car, whose only distinguishing feature is its bright orange-red color. The visual contrast with the truck is startling. When David first gets behind it on the highway, the first thing he notices is the obnoxious smoke pouring out of it and its blackened, greasy appearance. This typical, everyday occurrence quickly becomes a major conflict between the good guys—David and his cleanly designed automobile—and the bad guys—a smelly, highly flammable tank truck and its anonymous, uncontrollable driver.

Matheson's symbols of good and evil are animated by Spielberg's technical expertise. Using POV (point-of-view) shots, such as the "headlight" view of the road, Spielberg brings to life a machine that becomes an important ally to its conscious, human driver. The truck takes on the appearance of an evil personality. Since the driver of the truck is kept from sight, Spielberg lets us fantasize about the possibility that there is no driver at all, that an evil entity has taken over its controls to play cat and mouse with freeway drivers like David.

Carefully storyboarded, almost to the point of animation, the film reflects the influence of Chuck Jones's Road Runner cartoons. Just as in the cartoon, when David thinks he has outrun the truck, it appears again for another attack. (Pye and Myles point out the psychological parallel between the truck and other types of duelists in similar conflict: "The truck becomes alternately wolf, shark, tank, or prehistoric monster; it has a set of strategies from patient waiting to sudden strikes. It is the doom of Mr. Mann.")[5] One scene stands out for its cartoonlike depiction of domesticity. After being chased off the highway by the truck for the first time, David pulls into a combination gas station and laundromat. Once inside, he calls his wife—as if to touch base with reality by hearing a familiar voice—to apologize for an argument they had the night before. This domestic scene, shot through a "dryer window darkly," sets up David's character as mild mannered and nonaggressive. His wife berates him for letting an obnoxious man at a party "almost rape" her in front of everyone. (The wife is not particularly sympathetic; she looks as if she had stepped out of a television commercial for an oven cleaner. Wearing a dress and apron, she is vacuuming when the phone rings while two children play nearby on the floor with a toy robot.) As Pye and Myles note, "Mann has no answer for that. He asks himself: 'What did she expect me to do? Duel?'"[6]

Spielberg's exposition contrasts the absurd, irrational predicament David finds himself in to his middle-class suburban life. It is not surprising that in the beginning of the film, David constantly doubts that the faceless driver of the truck is actually trying to kill him. After a harrowing chase down a mountain grade—with the sun brightly shining and the black, sooty truck looking ominous with its snoutlike front—he drives into a fence in front of Chuck's Café.

At this point, David is convinced that he has fallen prey to a maniacal truck driver. He talks to himself as if to reaffirm his own existence and sanity. Two elderly men come out to see if he is all right and except for a neck injury, he seems to be fine. When he tells the old men that a truck was trying to run him off the road and kill him, they do not believe him because they do not see the truck. David quickly realizes that people around him think he's mad and suffering from delusions. He has only one alternative—to believe in himself and "duel." Pye and Myles note, "By now the social roles that define and support Mann have all collapsed. He does not rule his family, protect his wife, fight for himself, or help the children on the school bus; he lacks potency. He is deadened by his suburban life and aspirations. He becomes open prey— nudged onto a railway line in front of a train, trapped in a snake farm, allowed a brief respite by the roadside while he imagines the truck has gone on."[7] As soon as David is able, he goes inside the café. In the restroom, he washes up and tries to comprehend his incredible experience. In an interior monologue, echoed by the realistic sound of running water, he realizes how close evil is, that it exists, and that in spite of civilization, within minutes "we can be back in the jungle."

When he enters the service area of the café, he notices that the truck is parked in front. His fear is palpable as he looks at the ominous rig. Surveying the café, he considers the men in the room: any one of them could be his attacker. As he slowly inspects each one, he hopes to elicit a response from the guilty driver. Finding no sign or clue, he focuses on their feet looking for the telltale boots he spotted at the gas station. Upon finding a pair that look like the ones that got out of the truck, he foolishly confronts the driver and narrowly escapes being beaten. After the two are calmed by the café owner, the apparently innocent man departs in a huff and David is asked to leave. As he does, he sees the truck start up and begins chasing it on foot, which emphasizes his sense of terror and isolation against this unknown force.

He stops chasing the truck, which speeds away. He returns to his car, clears away the debris, and leaves. Once he is on the road again, everything appears normal, the truck no longer in sight. Here Spielberg employs the Hitchcockian device of allowing the evil or danger to pass momentarily. This allows the audience to catch its breath and also serves as a suspense-builder. During this interim pause David stops behind a schoolbus pulled off alongside the road. The driver explains that he needs a push, but David is uncertain whether his car will be able to accommodate the request. Spielberg's ability to portray children naturally is obvious here; the children act just as real ones would in the situation, making faces and gesturing at Mann through the rear windows. When the car does get stuck, Spielberg's sense of humor comes into play. Mann acts abnormally concerned about the hood of the car when the bus driver wants to jump on it to unhitch the bumpers.

The next scene is a beautiful shot of the truck framed by the mouth of a tunnel just ahead. When David sees it, he tries to make the driver and the children get back in the bus. They think him mad when the truck just sits ominously in the empty tunnel. As Pye and Myles describe it, "the truck waits for him at the end of the tunnel, its lights like animal eyes."[8] Then the truck slowly starts to move. It turns around, gets behind the bus, and helps to get it started. David, who had freed his car, watches in amazement.

David is next seen cruising along pastoral roads (birds chirp in the background) when the peace is broken by the sound of a train. When David stops at the railroad crossing, he is shocked to see the truck, which creeps up behind and attempts to push his car into the passing train. He barely escapes by driving across the track and up an embankment. The truck barrels past and David continues cautiously.

At the next opportunity, he stops to call the police at a gas station-snakearama. The truck returns from nowhere and rams into the phone booth just as David gets the operator. The truck wreaks havoc on the booth and the cages where the proprietress keeps her show snakes. David, now exhausted, climbs back into his car and tries to pull off the road to let the truck get far ahead. He dozes and in a lovely dreamlike sequence his thoughts flash back to the scene at the snake-arama. A train awakens him.

He finds the truck has also pulled off the road and is waiting for him. Two passersby refuse him aid and deny the situation; particularly uncooperative is an elderly couple that he flags down and asks to call the police. Although they want nothing to do with the matter, they get involved when the truck backs toward them.

David climbs back into the car and tries to outrun his pursuer on an upgrade. The pace quickens with corresponding musical intensity. Wide-angle shots of the eighteen-wheeler make it look as if it is floating. Meanwhile, we are privy to David's fears and see the road flying in front of him as if through his sunglasses. Spielberg uses close-up and quick-cutting shots of the speedometer, the gas pedal, and the rear-view mirror (a favorite visual object in his films) to intensify the drama. It becomes clear that any mistakes, whether human miscalculation or mechanical failure, will yield David to his closing foe. Spielberg employs the telephoto lens to compress the perspective making it appear that the ominous truck is only inches from David's rear bumper. When the radiator hose (he had been forewarned by the first gas station attendant) breaks, it looks as if the truck will claim its victim. Clouds of smoke pour from the underside of the car while panel instruments signal the problem.

In a last-ditch effort to save himself, David tricks his follower onto a byway. He jams his briefcase between the front seat and the gas pedal, aims the car toward the edge of a ridge, and jumps out. The truck, in heated pursuit with no time to stop, follows the car over the cliff. The truck crashes and bursts into flames.

Even now, Spielberg gives us no sign of human life within the truck. Extreme close-up shots dramatically reveal the result of the crash: steam coming from the truck's engine, a spinning left front wheel register the truck's slow, agonizing death. Spielberg even gives us a tour inside the cab. Papers and objects are seen on the dash. The only other clue that suggests a human driver is a small, black fan still running.

Looking over the cliff and down at the white ashes of his enemy, David is jubilant! He has won the duel.

It is evident from his achievement in *Duel* that Spielberg had found his niche as a promising director. His meticulous storyboarding, choice of lenses and shots, editing, and music all reveal his abilities not only as a filmmaker but also as a storyteller. The film also demonstrates the quick pace and rhythm evident in Spielberg's feature films, and it marks the first use of his favorite theme—ordinary people in extraordinary situations. Spielberg's David Mann is also Clovis and Lou Jean (*The Sugarland Express*), Chief Brody (*Jaws*), Ron Neary and Julian Guiler (*Close Encounters of the Third Kind*), Indiana Jones (*Raiders of the Lost Ark*), the children and mother in *ET*, and the Freeling family (*Poltergeist*).

After *Savage* in 1973, Spielberg's career as a contract television director was over. His feature-film career began with *The Sugarland Express* and the releasing of *Duel* theatrically in Europe.

A PERIOD OF TRANSITION

Locked into a seven-year television contract at Universal and waiting for his second television movie to materialize, Spielberg realized that he would have to take the initiative if he planned to work in feature films. During the lull in his work at Universal, he embarked on several projects, one of which he hoped would become a vehicle for his directorial debut.

One such project, *Ace Eli and Rodger of the Skies*, was written by Spielberg and submitted to David Brown and Richard

Zanuck, then at 20th Century–Fox.[9] His intention was to direct what he had written. Brown and Zanuck reviewed his previous material (several shorts and the television shows) and concluded that Spielberg was not ready to direct theatrical films. They did, however, buy the *Ace Eli* property, which was eventually directed by John Erman in 1973.

Shortly thereafter, Zanuck and Brown moved to Warners. Eighteen months later, they wound up on the Universal lot forming an alliance with Lou Wasserman, then head of Universal. Zanuck and Brown were given the opportunity to move the studio back into theatrical filmmaking as well as television. They were still considered independent producers, but all their feature films would be produced and distributed through Universal. It was at Universal that Spielberg finally gained their support and confidence.

Spielberg's television years found him directing his career as precisely as he directs films. After making his third television movie, *Savage*, Spielberg was given the opportunity to make his feature-film debut with *White Lightning*, a Burt Reynolds vehicle, since he had trouble at Universal getting *Sugarland* off the ground.[10] Spielberg spent almost three months on the picture, scouting locations and casting the movie until he realized it was not something he wanted to do for his first picture. Spielberg is quoted as saying, "I didn't want to start my career as a hard hat journeyman director. I wanted to do something a little more personal."[11] He wanted instead the *Sugarland Express* project to be his directorial debut in feature films. The timing of Zanuck and Brown's move to Universal was perfect; they agreed to produce *Sugarland*, thus affording Spielberg the opportunity to make his first theatrical motion picture.

Pye and Myles note, "After some thought Zanuck and Brown decided that they would back the project; but they cautiously buried it in their first batch of proposals."[12] Wasserman felt the script was "good," but realized the day of the anarchistic, antiestablishment "youth film" was over. Rather than posing obstacles for his new producing team, however,

Wasserman gave Zanuck and Brown the go-ahead on this low-budget film but warned, "Make the film, fellows. . . . But you may not be playing to full theaters."[13]

Spielberg's graduation to feature films brought with it a close association with the University of Southern California's class of 1967. Pye and Myles observe, "The members of that class were to become his closest associates in the film world. He would work from the same office building as John Milius; offer to share second unit duties on films by George Lucas; dream, with the others, of some final retreat to 'Shangri-Coppola,' where films are made without moguls or studios or interfering executives."[14] This collegial association began with the script for *The Sugarland Express*, which was written by two USC graduates—Hal Barwood and Matt Robbins.

"AMERICA ON WHEELS"

The title, *Sugarland Express*, refers to a train of cars moving toward Sugarland, Texas. A fugitive couple in a captured highway patrolman's car leads a procession of police, reporters, and curiosity seekers to their destination and tragedy. The "express" is the motivating force, literally and figuratively, for the film's plot.

Its appeal to young Spielberg is understandable, particularly after his success with *Duel*. He made the most of his expertise with machinery in *Sugarland*. Critics were impressed with the intricate maneuverings of the vehicles, which snaked gloriously across Texas—crashing, tipping over, or flowing across the screen—as the director willed. In his review, *Newsweek's* Paul Zimmerman praises Spielberg's "breathtaking command of action" and talks of his "vision, satiric but strangely beautiful, of an America on wheels."[15] He claims: "In this world the cars are as eloquent as the characters. . . . The pursuing police cars are like four-wheeled robots. . . . they hunt in packs and caravans, greedily sucking gas stations dry . . . crash into each other in acts of spectacular stupidity . . . [and] trail the trio with a prudence that borders on cowardice."[16] The cars are perhaps *more* eloquent than the characters, and that is a serious flaw in the film.

The film focuses on the characters in the lead car—the fugitives, Lou Jean (Goldie Hawn) and Clovis Poplin (William Atherton), and their hostage, Officer Slide (Michael Sacks). Based on a true story reported in newspapers in 1969, the plot depends on making the Poplins sympathetic, well-rounded characters. According to Tony Crawley, the actual fugitives— convict Robert Samuel Dent and his wife, Illa Faye—had become "instant folk-heroes" and their escapade "a media event."[17] In the film, however, Lou Jean and Clovis are not real, or likable, enough to win over an audience as *Bonnie and Clyde's* heroes did in 1967.

Lou Jean is the instigator of events in the film. She coerces her husband into running away from a minimum security facility, where he is serving a short term for a minor offense. Then she has him help her kidnap the highway patrolman to get his car. Hawn's performance received generally good reviews, but her stereotypical character is a weakness in the film. Spielberg's immaturity as a director is shown by his inability to make Lou Jean a more sympathetic character. She is a character out of the 1960s television series, "The Beverly Hillbillies," a member of a low socioeconomic class, lacking in education. In her comic moments, the audience is meant to laugh at her and not with her, and cruelly, to laugh at her because of her lack of sophistication and intelligence. It is an adolescent humor that probably served to establish Spielberg as a filmmaker who was better at directing action than characters. Interestingly, this is the most developed female character Spielberg had presented to that date.

Spielberg does do somewhat better with the male characters, particularly Captain Tanner, played by Ben Johnson. Tanner is the chief highway patrol officer, who insists on not harming the fugitives or their hostage. Johnson brings to his brief role a humanity, which Spielberg later realized would have strengthened the film had it been developed more fully.

He confesses: "That's one film [*Sugarland Express*] that I can honestly say if I had to do it all over again I'd make in a completely different fashion. The first half of the movie I would have played out the hand of Captain Tanner. . . . I would have drawn the whole first half of the film from his vantage point: from behind the police barricades, from inside his patrol cruiser. I would never see the fugitive kids, only hear their voices over the police radio, maybe see three heads in the distance through binoculars."[18] Such changes would have undoubtedly made *Sugarland* a stronger film. Again looking back, Spielberg admits:

> I don't think the authorities got a fair shake in [*Sugarland*] to know really why . . . the posse formed, why there was an overwhelming amount of vigilante activity and freestyle heroism, and why Capt. Tanner finally had to make the decision to put an end to this by destroying the characters in the car through force and violence. Capt. Tanner's decision is for me much too weak and unmotivated right now. I would spend the whole first half of the movie getting to know this man . . . why he valued human life so.
>
> Then the second half of the movie I would have told the entire story inside the car and how really naive and backwoodsy these people are and how frivolous and really stupid their goals were.[19]

It was Spielberg's view of Lou Jean and Clovis as "naive and backwoodsy" and their goals as "frivolous and stupid" that prevented their becoming viable characters, especially Lou Jean. Yet, he wanted his characters to seem as real and as "natural" as possible. In a 1982 interview, he claims to have done "a lot of printing of the early takes."[20] The role of the hostage, Officer Slide, is, like Tanner's, relatively strong. Sack's portrayal of how he begins to like and help his captors is believable, if slightly clichéd.

Spielberg's homage to the Road Runner cartoons is blatant and unabashed. To insure that viewers do not miss it, he has Clovis and Lou Jean watch a nearby drive-in theater screen on which Coyote and Road Runner enact their never-ending chase. Spielberg's symbolism is never subtle—he wants his audience to see the joke. This is perhaps one of his more endearing traits. He *likes* Road Runner and knows his audience does, too. If only he had liked Lou Jean and Clovis as well, *Sugarland Express* would have been a better film.

In spite of the problems with characterization, Spielberg's visual style (complemented by Vilmos Zsigmond's photography) and brilliant execution of the "escort" scenes provide a momentum for the audience that lasts until the climax: "the opening scenes are efficient, crisp."[21] Understandably, critics took notice. According to Alvin Marill, "Spielberg emerged recently from the ranks of Universal-TV's directors unit where he had established himself with the Joan Crawford segment of the original *Night Gallery* telefeature and latterly with the extraordinary neo-cultist *Duel*." He claims, "the premise [of *Sugarland*], played alternatively for comedy and drama, is basic fodder for a TV Movie of the Week—down to the slick Universal trappings.... However, [Spielberg] has proved himself much too creative to let his debut theafilm remain at this level and slowly molds an intelligent, engrossing movie chase, capturing striking bits of contemporary Americana...."[22]

The Sugarland Express did not lose money (it actually made a small profit after its sale to television), but Pye and Myles admit that there was something "wrong with the chemistry." Part of the problem was an ad campaign that changed several times in the hope that a workable marketing strategy could be found. In order to make the film more profitable, Spielberg was also willing to change the ending—letting his fugitives live—which would have been more consistent with Captain Tanner's character. However, this idea was rejected by producers Zanuck and Brown.

Carl Gottlieb, sensing Spielberg's dismay that *Sugarland* did not do well at the box office, attributed the film's lack of success to competition from two similar "youth movies": "Sometimes, the competition can work against everyone:

three well-made movies about outlaw couples on the run from organized society were released nearly simultaneously last year, by three different distributors/studios, and they all died—Steven's 'Sugarland Express,' Terry Malik's 'Badlands,' and Robert Altman's 'Thieves Like Us.' Any one of them might have had an individual success, but I think they split the ticket and divided the market, and everyone suffered."[23] Spielberg attributes the film's failure to its structure, which he now admits should have been different. In effect, he attempted to balance three parallel actions—all equal in weight, substance, and intensity—to tell his story. Spielberg is at his best with a linear storyline and one or two central characters. It is evident from his reworking of the *Jaws* script with Gottlieb that he intended to avoid this trap again, yet he committed the same mistake in *1941*, an overindulgent slapstick comedy, written by Robert Zemeckis and Bob Gale.

3 / Jaws:
"A Primal Scream Movie"

Spielberg managed to circumvent the old Hollywood adage "you are only as good as your last film" by lining up his next project before *The Sugarland Express* went into distribution. During the postproduction stages of *Sugarland*, Richard Zanuck and David Brown offered him the opportunity to direct *Jaws*.

In the summer of 1973, buoyed by the tremendous success of *The Sting*, Zanuck and Brown acquired the rights, including an option on a screenplay, to Peter Benchley's forthcoming novel about a New England coastal town terrorized by a great white shark. According to Carl Gottlieb, who cowrote the script and later wrote *The Jaws Log*, Spielberg first learned of Benchley's novel during his association with Zanuck and Brown on *Sugarland*.[1] After spotting the galley proofs in the Zanuck-Brown offices one day, he reportedly asked for a copy. Impressed by what he had read, Spielberg recalls, "I wanted to do *Jaws* for hostile reasons. I read it and felt that I had been attacked."[2]

Gottlieb writes that Spielberg was in Europe publicizing *Duel* when he was called to a meeting with Zanuck, Brown, and Peter Benchley in the south of France. There they discussed all the possibilities and problems of turning *Jaws* into a film. According to Gottlieb, "'Sugarland' had been a good experience for all concerned, and there was no reason to discourage anyone from becoming involved in the new 'Jaws' project."[3] When Spielberg expressed definite interest, Zanuck and Brown offered him the director's slot, pending contractual commitment. Universal Studios, meanwhile, was approached for development monies.

As the next step in Spielberg's career, this film was ideal. In many ways, *Jaws* was similar to his previous made-for-television movie *Duel*. A "director's movie," it offered him yet another chance to display his talents as an action director, although he was worried about becoming known as a "shark-and-truck" director.[5]

He need not have been concerned, for "at 27," Frank Rich notes, "director Steven Spielberg took a routine fish-bites-man story and transformed it into a show business phenomenon. *Jaws*, a merciless attack on the audience's nerves, quickly established its creator as the reigning boy genius of American cinema and went on to pile up the largest box office take in the history of the movies."[6]

FROM NOVEL TO SCREENPLAY

Not surprisingly, Peter Benchley was interested in writing the screenplay based on his novel. He is a third generation writer whose father, Nathaniel Benchley, had written an offbeat novel, *The Off-Islanders*, which became the basis for the feature film *The Russians Are Coming, The Russians Are Coming!*, and whose grandfather, Robert Benchley, had been famous in the 1930s for his comic writings, including several film shorts that he wrote and starred in. Benchley accepted a deal from Zanuck and Brown and promptly set to work on a first draft. After his second rewrite, Benchley bluntly states, "I lost the ego problem."[7] After his third draft, which incorporated many of Spielberg's suggestions, the script was submitted quietly to playwright Howard Sackler (*The Great White Hope*) for a rewrite early in 1974.[8] When Sackler's version was completed and deemed unacceptable, Spielberg asked Carl Gottlieb for assistance, fearing he would have to enter production without a finished shooting script. Gottlieb was a television writer and former comic actor.

Time reported that John Milius, a screenwriter, director,

and longtime friend of Spielberg, worked on the screenplay with Gottlieb,[9] but this conflicts with Gottlieb's book on the making of the film, which does not have Milius involved in any version of the screenplay.[10] (Gottlieb was initially only supposed to play the part of Amity's newspaper editor.)[11] After receiving the script, Gottlieb made up a list of criticisms and suggestions, which he returned to Spielberg. Finally, it was up to Spielberg and Gottlieb to rework the script on location.

The film that resulted was quite different from Benchley's novel and original screenplay. A *Time* magazine review claims: "Peter Benchley's novel spent too much time on dry land, plodding around Irving Wallace country, reinvestigating such tired phenomena as the uneasy marriage, the adulterous wife, the snaky seducer."[12] Benchley's political theme in *Jaws* is examined by reviewer Arthur Cooper of *Newsweek*: "Benchley aspired to some sort of commentary on society's venality in the confrontation between an insecure police chief who wanted to close the beaches after a couple of shark attacks and the town fathers who insisted on keeping the news from summer vacationers on whom the community preyed with sharklike cunning."[13] Spielberg and Gottlieb reduced Benchley's political statement to a subplot that was resolved by the end of the film's second act, leaving the third act free for the climax between man and shark.

According to screenwriter William Goldman, "In an adaptation, you have to make changes. In any adaptation, you simply must."[14] The changes Spielberg and Gottlieb made were essential, yet they captured the spirit of Benchley's marvelously visual opening—the terrifying attack on the young woman swimming alone in a dark sea. This is the vision Spielberg decided to "cling to."[15]

The basic storyline for *Jaws* deals with an enormous white shark that terrorizes the small New England coastal town of Amity. Spielberg and Gottlieb create three distinct acts that neatly unfold this story of horror. The film opens with a master shot of a nighttime beach party. A girl leaves the party with a young man to go swimming farther down the beach. She runs into the water, but the boy passes out on the shore. As she swims she is fatally attacked, and Amity is under siege.

When the body is discovered the next morning, the town's police chief, Brody, concludes that it is a shark attack and decides to close the beaches. He is soon persuaded by the town's mayor and newspaper editor, however, that it may not have been a shark attack and that the publicity would be bad for the summer tourist season just beginning.

After a boy is fatally attacked, a town meeting is called to discuss the situation. The mayor tries to calm everyone by insisting that the beaches are safe. The local sharkhunter, an eccentric named Quint, offers to rid the town of the menace for ten thousand dollars. The mayor takes his offer "under advisement."

The arrival of Hooper, an oceanographer and ichthyologist called in by Brody, begins the second act. Brody and Hooper begin investigating the attacks before the Fourth of July holiday, which traditionally brings an influx of tourists to Amity. After another scare, this time involving his own son Michael, Brody overrides the mayor and on the Fourth closes the beaches. The mayor approves hiring Quint to kill the shark.

The third act begins with Quint's acceptance of the job and his agreement to take Hooper and Brody along on the chase. After several harrowing experiences—and the loss to the shark of Quint and his craft, the *Orca*—the shark is killed and Hooper and Chief Brody swim ashore. Amity is safe once again.

PREPRODUCTION

During the planning stages, Spielberg and Joe Alves, the film's art director, looked at countless films featuring various aquatic creatures and monsters. They both decided they needed a more realistic "look" than had been achieved previously in a studio water tank. A decision was made to shoot on location at sea.

From the beginning, both Zanuck and Brown felt that the effects needed for *Jaws* were not beyond the range of Hollywood's talented special effects people. They even entertained the idea of a "trained" shark for the close-ups; both were amazed to find how little the experts knew about the species, much less a Hollywood animal trainer.[16] One plan, mentioned by Spielberg in an interview with Dick Cavett, was to use a short actor (Carl Rizzo) in the underwater close-ups with the shark. This proved impractical when on his test run Rizzo refused to go into the water with the sharks.[17]

When Spielberg and Alves concluded that a life-sized shark replica was needed, Alves made several clay models of the beast. Then he contacted Bob Mattey, who had been with Disney for seventeen years before retiring as head of their special effects department.[18] Mattey returned from semiretirement in response to this unusual request and brought the shark to life.

What Mattey created was a twenty-four foot, one-and-a-half ton polyurethane marvel—nicknamed Bruce early on. There were three versions of Bruce in all, each one costing approximately one hundred fifty thousand dollars. The first two mechanical sharks were designed for right-to-left and left-to-right movements on the surface of the water; the third, for underwater sequences. The mechanical structure of Bruce was an intricate network of hydraulic pistons and air lines utilizing compressed air for its operation.[19]

The operation of the mechanical shark was just as complicated as its inner workings. First a large steel platform containing controls operated by thirteen technicians in diving equipment had to be submerged to the ocean floor. From this platform a hundred-foot umbilical cord was connected to Bruce. This cord contained the control and air lines necessary to make Bruce function properly. During the initial run, Bruce sank like a rock; on the second attempt, the hydraulic system exploded.[20] These early complications projected long delays in the shooting schedule.

Roy Scheider, Richard Dreyfuss, and Robert Shaw were chosen to portray the three main human characters—Brody, Hooper, and Quint, respectively. The "smoothly corrupt but genuinely sincere" mayor was played by Murray Hamilton, one of the first actors hired.[21] Lorraine Gary as Brody's wife had the only other significant part in the film.

While Spielberg worked on the script, Alves was sent to scout locations. According to Gottlieb, he was looking for a place that would fit these "unique location requirements":

> an obvious summer resort town that derives 90% of its income in the 12-week summer season, full of picturesque and photogenic features. So far, easy. Now, recall the 12-ton steel submersible platform for the shark. This must operate in 25–35 feet of water, with a level, sandy bottom. Now you've got some limits to work within. But wait. In addition, there must be a sheltered bay in the lee of an island, so that the camera can point out to 180 degrees of unbroken horizon, and still be protected from vagaries of wind and weather, and mid-ocean swells. Further, the tide must be within manageable limits, preferably no more than two to three feet during normal seasons. . . . And, finally, all this natural beauty-sheltered anchorage, level sandy bottom, and optimum depth and tides—all this must be within 45 minutes drive or sail from a hotel complex capable of housing and feeding a feature film crew of over a hundred men and women, not counting stars and the above-the-line personnel like producers and directors.[22]

Alves discovered Martha's Vineyard, and Spielberg agreed it filled the requirements. Because of numerous unforeseen production problems, the beginning budget of $3.5 million doubled before the film was finished, and Spielberg was unable to leave the island for 155 days. Although some mechanical problems with the shark were anticipated, the logistics of shooting on location near and on the ocean was another matter altogether. A simple shot on the storyboard, such as a left-to-right movement by the shark grazing a boat, might have taken two days to shoot, but delays caused by the elements dramatically altered the situation. Unanticipated strong currents drew the equipment boats apart. Waves varied in size and rhythm, which caused the color of the water to change. Weather conditions over water created rapid changes in cloud patterns, and sudden rainstorms seemed to come out of nowhere.

The cast and crew occasionally went to the mainland to rest, but Spielberg refused to go. He felt that if he left Martha's Vineyard, he might never return. His determination, will, and spirit in continuing this picture appear to have taken on the same epic proportions as Captain Ahab's revenge toward Moby Dick, the great white whale who had robbed him of his leg, his friends, and his pride. Spielberg refused to be beaten by the incredible odds facing him.

Many reports and reviews of this period focus on Spielberg's ability to deliver the first-class product of a veteran film director despite his age and relative inexperience. *Newsweek*'s Arthur Cooper remarks, "despite his youth (27) Spielberg closely resembles those oldtime directors who disregarded the cerebrum and went right for the viscera. He is a virtuoso of action."[23] One has to consider, however, that it might have been Spielberg's youth that sustained him through the ordeal of *Jaws*. Other directors would have chosen to shoot all the aquatic scenes in a studio tank, probably a more sensible option, considering the complications of location work. However, in reminiscing about the pain and anguish involved in making the film, Spielberg recognizes: "I could have shot the movie in the tank . . . or even in a protected lake somewhere, but it would not have looked the same."[24]

STRUCTURAL ANALYSIS

Spielberg's continuously unfolding visualization of *Jaws*'s story is reminiscent of the storytelling techniques of Orson Welles, who, according to François Truffaut, "unlike Eisenstein and Dreyer, has never considered film as a plastic object but rather as a duration, something which unwinds like a ribbon."[25] Spielberg's most successful films have adhered to this straightforward storytelling method. Like Welles, who began his career in radio, Spielberg got his professional training in mass media—television. Like Welles, Spielberg has the ability noted by Truffaut "to set up aural bridges" and to use music "to capture or simulate awareness."[26] Coming from a visual medium, Spielberg also learned to set up "visual bridges" and to use action to move the story along quickly, as required in television production.

Spielberg has been quoted as saying he wanted *Jaws* to work as entertainment, to be a "primal scream" movie.[27] Through close daily editing with veteran film editor Verna Fields, he created a "movie" that combines classic elements of two film genres—horror and adventure.

The mise en scène is so tightly designed that certain critics, like William Pechter, have criticized Spielberg for having streamlined the principles of horror and adventure into a well-oiled "machine." According to Pechter, "*Jaws* is a fright machine to scare people."[28] Spielberg does have the ability to orchestrate all the elements of filmmaking—camera angles, lighting and textures, sound, and editing—to produce a highly entertaining and engaging film.

Spielberg himself characterized the film as strictly a "content" movie.[29] This might upset formalists who concentrate on form at the expense of content. Since Spielberg's films are visually stimulating and include a rich mixture of signs and symbols, one would expect the semiologists to delight in delivering interpretations. However, the signifiers and things signified in *Jaws* are presented in a straightforward linear pattern, seemingly without hidden meanings, symbolic icons, obvious metaphors, or intentional confusions.

The thematic meaning is certainly on the level of a child, which is where Spielberg wants it to be—on a childlike plane where we can be manipulated and catapulted into terror, where pure fantasy becomes believable. Spielberg's identification with childhood fantasy is another trait he shares with

Welles, who according to Andre Bazin, used the "fantasies of childhood" in many of his films.[30]

Childhood fears are an aspect of terror, according to Douglas Fowler: "The creator of terror art cannot make us afraid unless he returns us to our own childhood.... [Children] know that Under the Bed is deadly."[31] Spielberg confesses that he wanted to terrify people with the nightmarish thought of what lay under the surface of the water. The premise of *Duel* with the "driverless" truck, which represented the unknown, was applied to the shark, which represented the unpredictable.

With economy and lucidity Spielberg uses the opening shot of the nighttime beach party to set the time and place for *Jaws.* In the next scene, two of the partygoers, a young man and woman, run down the beach for an intimate swim. What begins as harmless fun soon turns into a nightmare when the young woman, who has left her drunken companion behind on shore, is attacked in the water. Although only the girl's nude body is seen thrashing in the murky water, it is an amazing visual realization of the powerful opening scene in Benchley's novel.

Wisely, Spielberg used the establishing shot to explain what would have been clear to a reader; thus, when the girl is attacked, there is no loss of momentum. This sequence is probably one of the most remembered and recognizable since the shower scene in Alfred Hitchcock's classic terror film *Psycho.* It exemplifies Spielberg's strong sense of visual style. Without gimmicks, or obvious special effects, he carefully applies the principles of terror.

The camera tracks police chief Brody (Roy Scheider) and his deputy as they discover the young woman's body in the early morning light. From this point, through the use of crowded sets, extras, a moving camera, and editing, the action picks up at a nervous pace. This pace is used throughout the film's first two acts and seems to propel the viewer toward a confrontation with the unknown.

Spielberg uses simple, but ingenious, touches to introduce

information about Brody early in the film. When he awakens at home—it is the morning after the attack on the girl—we learn he is married. Immediately, we find out he is not a native of the resort, when his wife (Lorraine Gary) makes fun of his obvious New York accent: "that's ya-a-d Martin, not yar-r-d." Not only does this establish Brody's foreignness, but it alerts the audience to the part of the country in which the film is set, New England. Spielberg depends on his visually and aurally literate audience (thanks to mass media and films) to pick up the clues and fill in the needed information. This technique is perhaps unique to Spielberg; he never "talks down" to his audience with tedious explanations but merely "knows" what they know. Throughout the film this helps to keep the pacing lively and to create surprisingly empathetic characters.

In a scene shortly after the body is found, Brody is shown trying to type the police report in a police station bustling with distractions. Spielberg is manipulating the audience by letting them in on Brody's excitement visually and aurally. A close-up of the hastily typed report in the typewriter reveals that Brody is terribly flustered (or a terrible speller) for he has typed "corner" for "coroner."

Later, in a contrastingly quiet scene in Brody's home, Brody is shown as a warm family man. As he sits rather detachedly drinking and contemplating events, his young son mimics his gestures with his glass of milk. This simple interlude continues until father and son playfully begin to make funny faces at each other. The scene serves to break the tension and lets the audience catch its breath.

Through these simple, but important scenes, Spielberg manages to convey details about the police chief that show him to be an insecure landlubber, the least likely person to claim victory over a monstrous killer shark. This is a switch from Benchley's novel, in which Mrs. Brody is the off-islander and her husband the native. Sadly, the wife's part suffers badly from this switch, as in the film she seems rather superfluous, existing only to provide symbols of home and family identification for Brody. Since she is the only significant woman in the film, one cannot use *Jaws* to assess Spielberg's ability to create viable female characters.

The seeming lack of complexity of the characters in *Jaws* has been noted by some reviewers and critics, but Jean-Pierre Coursodon disagrees: "The amount of intelligence Spielberg was able to bring to *Jaws*'s idiotic premise, especially in terms of characterization, was remarkable."[32] Spielberg was aided by a strong cast, as well as by the fact he took the time (rare in Hollywood film schedules) to rehearse the actors. Much of the dialogue in the film was improvised during these rehearsals. Spielberg is quoted as saying: "all the dialogue for *Jaws* came from improvisation because I was not one hundred percent happy with the script that I had developed and was responsible for. I was very happy with the structure, but not with some of the characterizations and dialogue. So I sat with these three talented actors at my house every day, and we improvised and rehearsed until we found a way to play the scene."[33]

Spielberg depends on costume and decor to provide an almost clownlike villain in the town's mayor, who is introduced when Brody, frantically buying materials for signs to close the beaches, bumps into him. Mayor Vaughn (Murray Hamilton) is comically decked out in a sportcoat festooned with anchors—obviously happily anticipating a prosperous tourist season. A scene on Amity's ferry is used to suggest the island's isolation and dependence on tourists for survival. The confining atmosphere of the ferry effectively shows the mayor and town leaders' avarice in forbidding Brody to close the beaches. Within minutes, Spielberg has transformed a comic figure into a villain made horribly dangerous because of a human failing—greed.

Scenes rush along creating a feeling of time passing rapidly, until an episode on the beach just before the Fourth of July holiday jamboree. The Fourth is Amity's big event; it is the day the beaches are officially opened for the tourist season. Long shots show what appears to be the town's entire population, including Brody and his family, out for the event. In a close-up, Brody is shown carefully scanning the horizon and waterline while everyone else is frenetically enjoying the beach.

Spielberg builds suspense in this sequence by manipulating shots of bathers splashing about in the water with gyrating leg movements photographed through underwater cameras, falsely hinting the shark's point of view. On the beach, the bathers are artfully reminiscent of American realist paintings—fat ladies in brightly colored swim suits, children with shovels and pails, and elderly men basking in the bright sunshine. Not surprisingly, Bill Butler, the cinematographer for *Jaws*, patterned the "look" of the scene on the photographic realism of Andrew Wyeth's paintings. He is quoted in *American Cinematographer*: "My philosophy for this film was that it should have an Andrew Wyeth look in the beginning, and as the story takes place around the Fourth of July, I wanted it to look sunshiny."[34] Butler's cinematography was totally successful in creating the "look" he aimed for. The scene was photographed using "a bevy of reflectors, augmented by three brute arc lights . . . set up to fill in the intensely strong sunlight."[35] Thanks to Butler's cinematic technique and Joe Alves's art direction, Spielberg's vision of the American scene successfully emerges on the screen.

Spielberg continues building the suspense amid all the aquatic activity by giving the audience a clue to coming events—a Hitchcockian shot of a dog swimming with a stick in its mouth. Several shots later, the dog is nowhere to be seen, only the stick floating atop the waves. In the distance, the dog's owner can be heard calling to it. Danger is obviously near, and Spielberg builds tension through the playful screams of teenagers. A close-up of Brody, still on the beach, shows him visibly more agitated. Finally, we see young Alex Kintner (Jeffrey Voorhees) afloat on his rubber raft. Spielberg takes us below for a suspense-building underwater shot where Alex's legs are vulnerably flapping off the back of the raft.

For the catastrophe in the next shot, Spielberg's camera is beached facing seaward; a long shot shows the raft turn upside down and a gush of red liquid spurts up. At this point, Spielberg introduces one of his favorite devices—the dolly-zoom. The effect is particularly harrowing: we see Brody still sitting on the beach in a medium close-up shot, while the background literally explodes outward from him. Spielberg uses this device to intensify Brody's reactions as he attempts to see exactly what is happening; it also creates a sense of isolation and helplessness when Brody is unable to respond fast enough to be of any help. "Did you see that?" remarks a vacationer to his wife basking in the sun. Brody, eyes wide, inches forward. There is another spurt of blood. Several screams are heard from the boy before he disappears from the camera's view. Brody leaps to his feet and yells for everyone to get out of the water.

This incident is not just another shark attack to build suspense, but becomes a pivotal point in the film. It concludes the first act and triggers events that will reveal the official cover-up in the second act and prepare the way for the seafaring adventure with Quint in the last. This knowledge of and respect for dramatic technique has made critics such as Pauline Kael claim that Spielberg is one of the few current Hollywood directors who know how to tell a story.

Spielberg uses the second act to introduce the other main characters, Quint and Hooper, as well as to resolve the conflict with the mayor. This act also contains humourous scenes that serve to lighten the tension and intensify the following scenes of horror.

Robert Shaw as Quint exhibits his Shakespearean background with a performance many critics felt to be excessive. He is introduced at a town meeting where he offers to rid the town of the beast, hoping presumably to collect the three-thousand dollar reward offered by the Kintner boy's mother. He plays the "old salt" to the hilt; his rather abrasive character is, according to Charles Derry, "introduced with one of those marvelous touches heretofore called Hitchcockian, but perhaps soon to be called Spielbergesque: the horrible sound of fingernails scratching against a blackboard." In his study of the modern horror film, Derry continues, this is "certainly one of the most horrendous sounds, almost universal in its ability to provoke sympathetic grimaces."[36]

Spielberg's childlike, mischievous sense of humor is apparent in this bit of juvenilia—for what young boy has resisted that old trick with the blackboard? But Spielberg uses the sound effectively to silence the commotion at the town meeting, for everyone, including the camera, zeroes in on the obnoxious noise and Quint.

Hooper, played by Richard Dreyfuss in a performance generally praised by critics, arrives in Amity amid a great deal of hustle and bustle. The townspeople have been mobilized; everyone seems to be jumping into boats to hunt the killer shark. Spielberg uses this portion of the film to provide some background on sharks. In a scene shortly before Hooper—an oceanographer and ichthyologist—arrives, Brody is seen at home researching shark attacks. Although Spielberg uses the book Brody is reading for a close-up of the mutilated victims of these attacks, he also inserts the reflection motif that so often appears in his early work. The pages of the book are reflected in Brody's glasses, projecting his thoughts on the horror.

The second act is enlivened by a comic scene in which two bumbling natives decide to capture the shark and collect the bounty. Sitting on a short pier they dangle a family's Sunday roast as bait. According to Gottlieb, it was a difficult scene to shoot. The actors were locals hired just for the scene and "although sincere in their efforts, they seemed unable to get things right" and Spielberg had to call for numerous takes.[37]

Spielberg cleverly executes the joke when the shark (never seen) grabs the bait, which is secured to a chain attached to the pier. The chain goes taut as the shark carries the bait out to sea and the men go into the water when the pier breaks apart. Although this scene is one of buffoonery, Spielberg capitalizes on it to build tension, because the audience is never sure if the two men will escape death. One of the men scrambles onto the remaining portion of the pier trying to help the other, who is swimming for dear life. The section of the pier floating out to sea turns abruptly around and begins chasing the swimmer. This is an example of the flexibility of Spielberg's directing techniques. Although a careful planner, he delights in the fortuitous accident that adds spontaneity to a film. Gottlieb notes that while shooting, "the man alternated between dying and surviving in various editions of the script; in the final version, we elected to play the scene for the terror of being in the ocean with the unseen monster."[38] The decision to opt for the positive outcome is a hallmark of Spielberg's films. He usually opts for "nice." As Richard Dreyfuss has remarked, "Look how nice his films are. . . . I mean they're nice."[39] This genuinely funny scene is unusual in the horror-thriller genre, because it lacks any feeling of the macabre. It is much more reminiscent of a Mack Sennett film than a monster movie. Although this is the longest sequence in the film played strictly for humor, humor is used throughout to create moments that relieve stress and manipulate the audience into relaxing before the next scene of horror.

Another example of Spielberg's humor occurs when Hooper and Brody decide to dissect a shark recently caught in local waters, thought by Amity's mayor and townspeople to be the killer fish. Hooper, insisting the shark is not large enough to have done all the damage, extracts a variety of digested material from the shark's stomach—including a Louisiana license plate. With a straight face, he claims this proves how far the shark must have traveled!

After the test screening, Spielberg felt a moment of terror was needed to balance the second act, so he added a scene that provided the biggest scare in the film. It occurs when Brody and Hooper go on a nighttime boat ride to hunt for the shark on the theory that sharks are "night feeders." They come across an abandoned fishing boat. Hooper investigates by diving into the water in scuba gear. Brody, who cannot swim, waits uneasily on the surface. The murky underwater shots provide claustrophobic tension while Hooper investigates a hole in the boat's hull. He finds a shark's tooth and, after examining it, goes in for a closer look. At any moment we expect the shark to spring forth and devour the ichthyologist like a gumdrop. Instead, Spielberg floats the head of the dead fisherman through the hole in the bow, scaring Hooper (and the audience). This sequence is beautifully executed by Spielberg in classic Hitchcock tradition. Spielberg recalls his motivation for adding the scene: "after this extraordinary preview in Dallas of *Jaws,* I still didn't feel I had enough reaction in the second act of the movie, so I designed the head coming out of the hole in the boat, which I shot in a friend's swimming pool. And that became the big scream of the movie. I felt the movie needed an explosive surprise at that point."[40]

The scene after Brody tells the mayor of their discovery shows tourists flocking to the beaches. The mayor has decided "the beaches will be open." Commercialism reigns. People are pouring into Amity from everywhere. The camera tracks the beaches, focusing in on a variety of body shapes and sizes—a technique reminiscent of Fellini's habit of surrounding his principal players with grotesque passersby. In the midst of all the frenetic activity, author Peter Benchley does a standup cameo as a television reporter, while a nervous Mayor Vaughn tries to coax some locals to go in the water to show the visitors all is well.

Spielberg often embeds movie memorabilia in his films. In this scene John Williams's score includes music from the crowd scene in John Ford's *The Quiet Man.* It is followed by a fanfare of ragtime music, possibly a tribute to Zanuck and Brown's recent hit, *The Sting.* The rest of the scene is played out—appropriately—to the tune "In the Good Ole Summertime."

Spielberg's films, as this scene in particular illustrates, depend upon well-defined camera positioning and movement. Jean-Pierre Coursodon has described Spielberg's visual style as "highly kinetic." He claims "Spielberg's camera, like his characters, seldom sits still. Movement is compulsive and often escalates to excited agitation, pandemonium, chaos—which is probably what Spielberg does best. He arranges for all hell to break loose and then delights in directing the traffic."[41]

The beach sequence ends with the bathers rushing from the water when an ominous fin is spotted. Spielberg shows the fin coming toward potential victims who register sheer horror. Just as guns are aimed at the menace from patrolling boats, the cardboard fin flops over and up come two young tykes attired in wetsuits and snorkles.

This scene is a clever distraction by Spielberg, for the "real" shark fin is soon spotted on the other side of the bay, where Brody's son Michael and a playmate are boating. The shark attacks a man in a boat nearby. The turbulence capsizes Michael's boat, throwing him and his playmate into the water. He is immobilized by fear. Still unseen, the huge shark seems to brush the boy before it leaves the cove. This incident is capsuled in a hospital confrontation with the mayor, who finally agrees to authorize a shark hunt. Act 2 is over.

Act 3 is the sea adventure. And what an adventure it is. Spielberg's flair for action direction takes over. The scenes were shot laboriously in sometimes rough seas, and the texture and lighting are gloomy and foreboding, successfully adding to the atmosphere of confinement and waiting. The hand-held camera work by Michael Chapman, working with director of photography Butler under Spielberg's watchful direction, adds a feeling of cinema verité uncommon in standard horror or adventure films.

Spielberg slows his energetic mise en scène to introduce motivation for the characters, including Quint's seemingly maniacal desire to hunt the shark. In an improvisational-style storytelling session in the *Orca's* cabin, the three protagonists reveal their personalities. Brody is shown to be the real hero of the piece, because he has gone out to hunt the shark in spite of his acknowledged fear of the water and his inability to swim. Under Spielberg's direction, Brody's growth is believable; he seems terribly vulnerable but bravely willing to do what needs to be done. The cramped, swaying cabin brings out Brody's fear and emphasizes the feeling of isolation and "confinement" that critic Douglas Fowler feels essential to the horror genre. According to Fowler, "when the inherent power of film to take us into a scene is combined with a story in which confinement is of the essence, the effect is a little short of harrowing. . . . *Jaws* was an effective horror film largely because Spielberg understood how to use his medium to achieve both a sense of mystery and a sense of confinement."[42]

Mystery is further enhanced through the development of Quint's character. Robert Shaw's portrayal of Quint is, according to Edith Blake, based on a real islander, an eccentric seagoing type whose stories and accent were studied by Shaw.[43] This resulted in a performance that Marcia Magill describes as a "curious one. He comes on overly strong, larger than life."[44]

On board the *Orca*, Quint's mysterious motive is revealed. Spielberg uses medium two-shots of Quint and Hooper, which links them as experienced seamen comparing scars and sea tales. In the process—which omits Brody, further emphasizing his lack of knowledge and isolation—Quint reveals that his desire to kill sharks is for revenge. He recounts a hideous World War II incident in which he and eleven hundred shipmates, on a ship returning from delivering the atom bomb dropped on Hiroshima, were torpedoed and left to swim helplessly in shark-infested waters. This reference to the atomic bomb is a motif typical of the horror genre and Spielberg uses it to foreshadow Quint's demise. As Charles Derry notes, "As soon as we hear Quint's story, we know that he must die. The shark is inevitably returning to finish the job left undone that day in 1944 [*sic*] in the Pacific; only after Quint is punished and destroyed (for his role in delivering the bomb?) can the shark be vanquished."[45]

The scene that follows, where the men aboard the *Orca* sing searfaring chanties, serves to break the heavy mood set by

Quint's story. This is a typical Spielberg tactic—he rarely lets the pace slow for long. In a long shot, the *Orca* is seen resting quietly on a moonlit sea while the sound track echoes the faint song from the vessel. In almost cartoonlike fashion, reminiscent again of Chuck Jones's animations, a yellow barrel, attached to the shark in a previous bout, pops up unexpectedly in the frame's foreground, hesitates, and then zips merrily across the water towards its intended target—the *Orca*. John Williams's four-note score quickens in pace and intensity until the moment the shark rams the vessel. The men are stunned by the jolt and silently question its origins. Seconds later, the shark rams the boat again, breaking several planks in the hull. With the attacker clearly identified, they jump to their feet to retaliate.

Spielberg establishes a realistic terror through long shots of the shark attacking the *Orca*. Underwater scenes of real shark footage shot by Ron and Valerie Taylor were flawlessly edited into the film by Verna Fields.

On location at the Vineyard, she and Spielberg successfully honed the first two acts of the picture while the third act was being filmed. After the location filming on Martha's Vineyard was completed, Fields installed her flatbed editor in a poolhouse at her home ready to edit the third act. According to Gottlieb, this was not an easy job, because slates listing scenes were confused or incorrect and shots were included that were not in the script.[46] This confusion was partly due to Spielberg's improvising most of the third act, which he had to do in order to work around the problems of the mechanical shark and the unpredictable elements. Some scenes that follow one another in the final edit were shot months apart. In order for Fields to make sense out of these shots, she had to rough out a continuity by going through each clip to see where it might fit in. Weather conditions changed quite frequently, even within a day's shooting, thereby giving Bill Butler's photography visual discontinuity. Fields had to cut around the obvious contradictions in the weather. She did this by using high camera angles whenever possible—so the sky would not be seen too much—and by cutting close on the action—so the audience would concentrate its attention on the characters and the horror of the situation rather than on the changing background. They even discussed desaturating the color in the sea adventure scenes to intensify the gloominess and further distract from the changing cloud patterns in the sky. After Fields assembled the third act, Spielberg went through her initial cut, scene by scene, substituting shots that worked better. After this session, Fields then made the fine cut, tightening up the action even more.

The terror of the sea adventure scenes is enhanced by John Williams's Oscar-winning musical score. Spielberg worked closely with Williams to obtain the right musical mood for these scenes. In an interview on ABC's "20/20," Williams playfully demonstrates how the shark's movements could appear to speed up or slow down through the rhythm of music.[47] Spielberg's orchestration of the elements of a scene effectively incorporates Hitchcockian techniques, such as the device of playing hide-and-seek with the audience. By adhering to this strategy—now you might see it, now you don't, now you almost do, and you won't until the end—Spielberg successfully creates the illusion of ultimate terror.

Hooper is lowered in a shark cage with a spear gun tipped with poison in a last-ditch effort to kill the shark. Spielberg uses spellbinding footage of a real shark off the coast of Australia photographed by the Taylors to enhance the scene. Carl Rizzo, a former jockey standing only four feet eleven inches, is photographed underwater in a miniature shark cage to create the illusion that a real shark in the scene with him is much larger than it actually is. Because the size of the real shark appeared proportional to Bob Mattey's mechanical shark, the two scenes could be easily intercut to enhance realism. The shark's attack on the cage causes Hooper to drop his spear gun, forcing him to escape through the twisted bars when the shark retreats momentarily. He quickly swims to the ocean floor where he hides in a coral reef to escape the shark's fury. On deck, meanwhile, Brody and Quint are aware of the shark's attack on the cage, and desperately try to retrieve it. They eventually raise it from the ocean, but the battered shark cage is empty and Hooper is feared dead.

The scene in which the shark finally appears in full view, an obligatory one in the horror genre, is skillfully done. The obviously mechanical shark is shown as briefly as possible (although many reviewers felt not briefly enough!), while a close-up focuses on blood spurting from Quint's mouth as he is devoured by the shark. Hand inspection of the frames reveals that Spielberg used subliminal "ghosting," a technique by which shadows of objects are double-exposed in the scene: a flurry of shark fins quickly dash about in the corners of the frame as Quint is being eaten by the huge fish.[48]

The scene recalls the biblical story of Jonah and the whale, to which Melville makes reference in *Moby Dick*. Quint is killed by the huge creature of the sea, just as Jonah and Captain Ahab are confronted by giant whales. Most of the similarities between *Jaws* and *Moby Dick* (or at least John Huston's film version of the latter) appear in this final act. Spielberg and Gottlieb's characters bear a slight, but deliberate, resemblance to the revengeful Captain Ahab (Quint), the inexperienced young mariner, Ishmael (Brody), and the knowledgeable Queequeg (Hooper). (Spielberg enhanced Benchley's novel by adding the element of revenge as a motivation for Quint.) Particularly reminiscent of Huston's film is a scene on the *Orca*'s deck in which Quint teaches Brody to tie seaman's knots while a bored Hooper plays solitaire (fortune-telling?), awaiting his fate. In the Houston film, Queequeg is shown casting his small animal bones to foretell the future. Again, Spielberg is depending on the filmic literacy of his audience, many of whom would be familiar with the film of *Moby Dick*. To those who are aware of the parallel, the echoes add a sense of recognition and fun. On the other hand, for anyone not familiar with the film, there is enough in Spielberg's mise en scène to provide complete satisfaction. Thus, the sea adventure operates on two levels, a storytelling technique employed in Spielberg's later films.

With Quint's demise, only Brody is left to do battle with the shark. After several attacks on the boat, Brody manages to lodge one of Hooper's diving tanks in the shark's mouth. With the boat now completely underwater except for the mast—which Brody clings to for life—the shark begins its final attack. Armed with his rifle, Brody carefully aims it at the oncoming shark, screaming, "Smile, you son of a bitch!" He fires and hits the air tank, which explodes violently and tears the shark to pieces. Brody heaves a sigh of relief, but is given a deathly scare when Hooper miraculously appears from the water. Hooper inquires about the fate of Quint, but Brody merely shakes his head.

Spielberg's penchant for "niceness" is displayed in the scene when the two survivors, Brody and Hooper, head for shore on a makeshift raft. The *Orca* had been obligingly pointed homeward by Spielberg before it was sunk, giving the audience hope that a happy ending would ensue.

JAWS: THE PHENOMENON

Spielberg is reported to have been the only member of the *Jaws* crew not to leave Martha's Vineyard once location shooting began (shooting was originally scheduled to last two to three months, ending just before the real tourist season on Martha's Vineyard began; however, filming stretched out over five months before it was completed). As Spielberg pulled away on the last day, according to Gottlieb, he yelled, "I shall not return!"

He could not then have been aware of the effect the film would have on his career. Hollywood loves a blockbuster and within a very short time of its release date in the summer of 1975 *Jaws* broke all previous box-office records and earned Spielberg increased critical notice. According to industry reports, *Jaws* was the first film in the history of motion pictures to gross over $100 million on its initial run. It was a record not to be broken until the release of George Lucas's *Star Wars* in 1977.

Jaws really began a "renaissance" for the Hollywood film. Spielberg and Lucas were the guiding forces in "a rebirth and a revolution in the art of Hollywood" just as, Bazin notes, Orson Welles (with *Citizen Kane*) had been for the postwar period.[49] *Jaws* captured four Academy Award nominations, including one for Best Picture of the Year, but Spielberg was not nominated in the Best Director category. It was a disappointment, considering the fact that he felt *Jaws* was a "director's movie."

4 / Close Encounters's "Mr. Everyday-Regular Director"

After chasing cars and sharks to critical and financial success, Spielberg turned skyward for inspiration. Unlike George Lucas's adventure in space, *Star Wars*, however, Spielberg's 1977 space opera is also earthbound. He drew upon his boyhood interest in space, his previous amateur film, *Firelight*,[1] and existing research on unidentified flying objects to create *Close Encounters of the Third Kind*. With this film Spielberg achieved Frank Capra's highly coveted "name above the title" in the credits, where he is listed as both writer and director. His "breakout film," it established Spielberg as an upcoming superstar within the industry and earned him critical acclaim as a wunderkind.

While Spielberg was filming *Jaws*, he not only feverishly worked with Gottlieb on the revisions of the script, but he also managed to develop an unusual UFO story for his next film. Spielberg was careful to refer to this project as an "adventure thriller," because the "sci-fi" label would be hard to sell to studios (Spielberg's friend and colleague, George Lucas, was trying to sell Twentieth Century–Fox on the *Star Wars* idea at about the same time, with similar difficulty).[2] Pye and Myles note, "However fascinated the American public might be with the possibility of alien life, the arithmetic was against a multi-million dollar investment in those dreams."[3] Although Columbia was in financial trouble, it agreed to make *Close Encounters* for the following reasons: the strength of *Jaws*'s success, the producing team of Julia and Michael Phillips (*The Sting*, 1974, and *Taxi Driver*, 1976), and a financial arrangement that spread out the risk for the studio.

Close Encounters, inspired by the song "When You Wish upon a Star" from Walt Disney's *Pinocchio,* illustrates the strong suburban roots in Spielberg's films. It is a turnabout from the typical fifties sci-fi flicks that usually featured aliens as villainous creatures attempting to take over planet Earth. Spielberg's innovative approach was to create oddly appealing creatures from outer space who come to Earth to learn about our planet rather than to destroy it.

Spielberg's idea for a UFO movie originally had its roots in his two-and-a-half hour amateur effort, *Firelight,* which he made when he was sixteen. The film dealt with an invasion of hostile aliens from another planet. Much later, Spielberg became interested in the details surrounding Betty and Barney Miller, a couple who claimed they were abducted by aliens for a few hours while on their way home from a vacation trip.[4] Tony Crawley reports that the script of *Close Encounters* grew out of Spielberg's short story "Experiences," which he wrote while working as a television director for Universal: "His setting back then was, naturally enough, a small mid-Western township. On its Lovers' Lane, the necking teens in jeans—skipping from working for his teenage films?—got to see what he always missed. A UFO light show in the night skies. He liked it. He thought the story went well with Jiminy Cricket's 'When You Wish Upon A Star.'"[5]

Spielberg had first come up with a sketch called "Watch the Skies," which he presented to David Begelman at Columbia; that script featured a United States Air Force officer frustrated at having to cover up UFO sightings for the government. Michael and Julia Phillips, who produced *Close Encounters,* suggested screenwriter Paul Schrader to rework Spielberg's story. It was Schrader who came up with the title, *Close Encounters of the Third Kind,* but Spielberg was quite upset with Schrader's script. Crawley notes, "In a word, Spielberg *loathed* it. . . . he felt the script was a typically Calvinist tract from Schrader, [had] little to do with UFOs, *nothing* to do with Spielbergian UFOs."[6] Finally, Spielberg's screenwriter friends Hal Barwood and Matt Robbins (*Sugarland Express*) were brought in to work on the script. The result is a science-fiction film with unprecedented special effects, which, as Steven C. Early notes, is also "about people."[7]

The film, originally budgeted by Columbia Pictures at eight million dollars, was shot on location at Devil's Tower in Gillette, Wyoming; in several converted hangars located at Mobile, Alabama; in the Mojave Desert, and in Bombay, India.[8] After the success of *Jaws*, Spielberg was able to command the services of some of Hollywood's (and Britain's) greatest artists and technicians to bring his special effects concepts to the screen. Douglas Trumbull, who had done the special effects for *2001: A Space Odyssey* and *Star Wars*, was contracted. Both Trumbull and Spielberg carried special effects to new heights, even for Hollywood. The space ship featured in the film became a brightly lit, magical floating palace. The film's complexities required the efforts of three noted cinematographers—Vilmos Zsigmond, William A. Fraker, and Douglas Slocombe—as well as a large crew of technicians and the expertise of producer Julia Phillips. Michael Kahn served as editor and Joe Alves (*Jaws* and *Sugarland Express*) was once again in charge of production design. John Williams, who had won an Academy Award for his score in *Jaws*, supplied highly effective and memorable music for his third Spielberg film.

According to Pye and Myles, "*Close Encounters of the Third Kind* was a surprising project for Columbia. The corporation was convalescing after a nearly fatal financial crisis. . . . The studio itself had strictly limited resources."[9] Columbia's strategy was to sell the film as a forthcoming blockbuster. As a result, the up-front money received from theaters was the highest to date, but with no guarantee of exclusivity; in addition, Columbia also requested two thousand dollars from each theater for promotional costs. The scheme worked, bringing in a total collection of over twenty-four million dollars in advance payments, a figure higher than the actual cost of the production. Columbia had a lot riding on the film. Many industry sources predicted a dire fate for the company, if this film, a tricky venture at best, failed at the box office. To complicate matters, two film reviewers sneaked into a restricted test preview of the film at a Texas theater in October 1977, and gave it a bad review. This sent negative shock waves through the theater community, which had bid on the film in August for fall release. Even John Milius noted, "it will either be the best Columbia film or it will be the last Columbia film."[10]

Several locations were scouted for large buildings to serve as sets for the production—even considered were the Goodyear Blimp hangar and the Houston Astrodome. Finally, four large hangars were found on a deserted Air Force base in Mobile, Alabama. The hangar that contained the Box Canyon locale became affectionately known by cast and crew as the "big set."[11] This set served as the staging area for the meeting between humans and aliens. Another large hangar was used for several small sets, such as the "Crescendo Summit" set, where Roy Neary almost runs over Barry with the power company truck.[20]

As with *Jaws*, Spielberg tried to maintain a high degree of secrecy on the set. His fears probably stemmed from his training in television, where rip-off movies-of-the-week, which can be shot in less than twenty days, sometimes beat the release date of the motion picture on which it is patterned. *American Cinematographer* reported that tight security was necessary to "protect the dramatic concept, the impact of the story, and the special visual photographic effects."[12] The "big set" was so guarded that cast and crew were required to present I.D. badges before they were allowed in. On several embarrassing occasions, security guards refused Dreyfuss entry because he forgot his badge.

STRUCTURAL ANALYSIS

The film begins in medias res; a group of men is making its way through a desert in a swirling dust storm.[13] The figures come upon abandoned World War II fighter planes and register great surprise. In a style reminiscent of early silent movies, they convey the excitement of a great discovery.[14] François Truffaut, as Lacombe, is first glimpsed in this rather chaotic scene, which features subtitles.

Incongruously, the crew then encounters an old man sitting alone on the porch of a wooden shack. The old man makes little sense: he looks skyward and mumbles an incredible story of the sun coming out in the dead of night and singing to him. His unusual experience is interpreted to Lacombe by an American crew member, David Laughlin (played by Bob Balaban, who later wrote a book about his experience), after it is translated into French for Laughlin by another member who questions the old man in Spanish! The entire episode is confusing, including the use of subtitles. *Newsweek* reviewer Jack Kroll comments, "Truffaut's dialogue, crucial to the exposition, switches from English to French," which "gives the film an international aura but can be irritating. Some of the overlapping dialogue, inspired by Orson Welles and Robert Altman, also gets blurry."[15]

This is not the beginning Spielberg had originally planned for *Close Encounters*. It does, however, effectively create an air of excitement and shows the worldwide fascination of man (literally of "man"—there are no women among the international investigating team) with the mysteries of the universe. The opening scenes, added after production of the film had supposedly ended, are an example of Spielberg's skillful film rhetoric. He stages these international sequences like television news coverage of world crises, identified as such by his television generation audience and thus accepted as credible.

The episodic structure of the film permitted Spielberg to drop in this beginning without altering the progress of the story, which shifts between such international scenes of unexplained events and the ordinary, everyday lives of two families—the Nearys and the Guilers—in Muncie, Indiana. It also serves to introduce Truffaut's character early in the film.

Despite Early's claim that *Close Encounters* "is about people,"[16] the characters in the film, including Lacombe, are closer to types or symbols. Spielberg admits that his films are often larger than the characters.[17] *Close Encounters* is a classic example of the modernist landscape that Spielberg so often paints in his films. The characters are there to react to events, not to guide them. What they lack in depth they make up for in audience recognition (another effect of Spielberg's rhetorical technique). Delineated with a deft touch and Spielbergian humor, Roy Neary and his family are stock figures; they are even costumed from a book of photographs of real middle-class Americans.[18]

Just as the characters in *Jaws* are subservient to the action, so are they in *Close Encounters*. This technique is not unique to Spielberg but is typical of recent American fiction. As Raymond M. Olderman notes in his essay on American literature of the midseventies, fictional characters of this period are typically "not static ideals or individual psychological studies; they are *representative characters,* composite people who are assembled from the norms of a particular community of people."[19] Spielberg's characters are part of the zeitgeist of the seventies; the product of the sixties' deep social change, they live in a faster-signified world, propelled by television to expect instant recognition. But Spielberg's unique touch makes more of "less" in characterizations. Within a few frames he establishes clearly identifiable (if not stereotypical) characters representative of suburbia. His characters do not take away from the action, but are merely there to be swept up by it.

Using such characters, Spielberg moves from the dusty desert to an air traffic control tower where an unidentified flying object is present on the radar screen. The scene is purposely played low key and emotionless, reflecting Spielberg's fascination with "professionals," scientists, and authority figures presented as objectively cold and calculating types. It also establishes how unorthodox incidents are handled by professionals: intently pursued, looked upon skeptically, and finally, largely ignored. After the UFO makes a pass at one of the planes, the controller asks the pilots if they want to file a report; both respond negatively and the whole matter, handled routinely, is dropped.

The next scene reveals a small house on the isolated outskirts of Muncie, Indiana. A black murky sky is clouding over ominously.[20] Inside the house, a single mother, Jillian Guiler (Melinda Dillon), and her four-year-old son Barry (Cary Guffey) are asleep. Clanking cymbals wake the boy, who pops out of bed to investigate toy trucks and cars that are mysteriously zooming about while a record player blares. Jack Kroll, in his *Newsweek* review, compares the scene to the beginning of Stanley Kubrick's film *2001*. He claims, "Kubrick's image was apocalyptic, magnificently pretentious. Spielberg's is also full of portent, but it's friendly, domestic and touchingly whimsical."[21]

Barry walks into the kitchen, where the mysterious force is wreaking havoc. The refrigerator door opens and food pours out all over the floor, glasses and dishes fall from cabinets while furniture rocks violently back and forth. A calmly curious Barry views the chaos: Spielberg uses the scene to show the division between children, who are accepting and loving, and adults, who remain skeptical. Only the adults are scared in this film.

Barry's mother is finally wakened by a toy police car that makes its way into her room, its siren blaring. She goes to investigate, her son obviously her first concern. Jillian hears him talking from outside the house and looks out the window. Barry seems to be following something into the woods. Jillian runs downstairs (fully dressed—conveniently she sleeps in her gym shorts) to pursue her son's odd excursion into the night.

The action jumps to the Neary household. Roy Neary (Rich-

ard Dreyfuss) is a power company employee who has an un-
nerving experience with UFOs and develops an obsessive
need to find them. Here Spielberg returns to his real roots—
suburbia. Roy lives in a middle-American, Sears-decorated,
thin-walled tract home with his wife, Ronnie (Teri Garr—
who, according to Bob Balaban, wanted to play the part of
Jillian rather than Roy Neary's wife), and his three less-than-
perfect children. Family life is chaotic, even before Daddy
tries to relive his strange experiences by sculpting mountainlike shapes out of his mashed potatoes and shaving cream.
Such details show Spielberg's identification with "real life"
in lower middle-class America. The half-gallon cardboard
milk carton is always on the dinner table; the television is
always on; Daddy has more toys in the "family room" than
the children (a train setup nearly covers the room), and UFOs
fly past McDonald's.

In one comic scene, Dad tries to teach his oldest child frac-
tions. Roy employs the toy train for the tutorial. As the train
zooms around the tracks toward a box car sitting in the middle of an intersection, Roy asks his son what fraction of the
box car needs to be moved out of the way before the oncoming
train hits it. The son stumbles for an answer, but the train
smashes the box car head on. With Roy and son both frustrated, the suburban lesson ends in failure.

His wife then informs him that he promised to take the children to a movie. Roy suggests Walt Disney's *Pinocchio* (during one of its many revivals); but the kids want to play goofy
golf instead of seeing a "dumb cartoon." Spielberg's references to Disney appear throughout the film, as do frequent
tributes to other classic films and noted filmmakers. The Disney echoes suggest the chameleon effect Spielberg wants—for
the adults to become kids again and experience wonder, mystery, and fascination. Roy is propelled toward his alien rendezvous because he is just a big kid. At times his "adult"
behavior—with all its middle-class trimmings—takes over,
but not for long.

The phone rings and Roy is called to duty by the power

company: there is a power outage. With his company truck, armed with all the tools necessary to restore power, he sets out to find the malfunctioning substation. Spielberg's use of comedy, coupled with Dreyfuss's natural acting ability, creates a "sweetness" that belies earlier charges that Spielberg pays more attention to mechanical effects than characters.[22] Roy stops at a railroad crossing to scan his road map. A car pulls up behind him, headlights glowing. Roy waves the car to go around him. Still charting his position, another "car," with "headlights" on high, pulls up behind him. Again he waves the car to go around him, paying less attention to it than the last one. Rather than going around him, the "headlights" rise upward. A series of roadside mail boxes explode open and shake back and forth violently. He turns on his flashlight to take a look, but the light dims and eventually goes out altogether. Then his truck goes completely dead. A bright searing light from above descends upon the truck, as if inspecting it. Roy looks out of his cab window toward the light but it is too bright. The railroad crossing lights become activated, the bell goes off, and both signs begin to shake violently back and forth. Havoc breaks out in Roy's cab—papers fly everywhere defying gravity, lights flicker on and off, electrical gauges on the dashboard begin to burn up. Roy sits in awe until the light disappears. A large object moves over him and down the road scanning the surface of the asphalt with its intense, searing beam of light. When the object finally disappears, Roy's truck restarts automatically. He puts the truck in gear and begins frantically to follow the object.

Driving recklessly, Roy rounds a curve and almost hits a small child. It is Barry, who is clutched from injury at the last minute by his mother. The truck veers and crashes into a guard rail, coming to a stop. After checking that Barry is all right, Roy looks around at the people who are gathered on the hillside overlooking Muncie. They are obviously waiting to see something or waiting for something to happen. An odd collection, they recall the people "affected" by aliens in 1950s sci-fi films—they appear mesmerized, almost zombielike, waiting for the aliens to come. Roy and Jillian walk to the side of the road when bright lights swirl around a curve. The onlookers watch in amazement. A procession of larger alien craft is followed by a small red ball of light that Jack Kroll astutely recognizes as "a classic Disney device—a little red UFO that comes skittering along after the bigger ships is the old Disney gag of the last little dwarf or chipmunk stumbling after his dignified elders."[23]

Next appear several police cars chasing the alien craft. Roy joins the chase, leaving Jillian and Barry behind. Spielberg plays the chase for gags by having a lonely toll gate come to life seemingly by itself. But the alien craft have gone through, setting off the alarm. The attendant awakes in confusion only to see the police cars follow. "Hey, that'll cost you a quarter," he says. No one bothers to stop and inform him of the circumstances. When the alien craft soar off a cliff and fly skyward, the lead police car—suggestive of one in a Harold Lloyd comedy—mindlessly follows in pursuit, crashing off the cliff. Several other police cars, as well as Roy's truck, come to a stop before plunging to a similar fate. The alien craft zoom out over the horizon and toward the heavens like a trio of fighter jets breaking formation. Peering out into the darkness, Roy and the police see the lights of the city come on section by section.

Roy rushes home to wake his wife and kids. He wants them to see what he has seen. They think he is delirious but drive back with him to Crescendo Summit where he had almost run over Barry. They wait for something to happen, but nothing does. A frustrated Ronnie remarks how she used to come to places like this to "make out." This remark, geared to Spielberg's youthful audience, is about as close a reference to sex as there is in the film.

The action cuts to the Gobi desert where the international team is pursuing another find—a lost ship that has reappeared in the desert. This was one of the additional scenes that Spielberg shot for the special edition, a reedited version of the film released in 1980. It is a magnificent shot, but many critics accused Spielberg of throwing in for the sake of spectacle. Yet Spielberg enjoys "spectacle"; these kinds of shots stand out in Spielberg's memory as a moviegoer. He feels that spectacle creates movie magic; indeed, the most memorable scenes in his work are those that lean toward spectacle and recall other films.

Spielberg instantly switches again—like changing a channel on a television set—to the Neary home. Roy's wife, Ronnie, is concerned about his burned face. His son says it looks like a "50-50" candy bar, but Mom is more concerned about what the neighbors will think—a typical middle-class reaction. As Roy squirts shaving cream into his palm, he begins to shape the cream into a mountainlike structure. He is not sure what it means and asks his wife if it reminds her of anything. She looks at him with a leary eye and is upset when he wants to tell others about his UFO experience. The phone rings and Ronnie answers it. She sounds troubled. When she hangs up, she tells Roy he has been fired from his job; company officials did not even want to talk to him. Roy flippantly throws this off by saying he can get another job.

Spielberg here injects another international scene, where Lacombe and fellow researchers are investigating chanting Indians pointing toward the sky. Their chant is the famous five-note melody that John Williams created for the film. Lacombe's team is busy recording the sounds with tape recorders, which in the next scene he demonstrates to fellow scientists in a large auditorium. He believes the tones to be a form of communication.

Roy goes to the mountain again, where he meets Jillian and Barry. They begin exchanging stories about their experiences when Roy notices Barry building a mountainlike structure. He leans over the child commenting on its significant shape. Almost immediately, someone screams that the aliens are coming out of the Northeast. The patient UFO watchers stand up to greet the aliens, some holding signs while others offer friendly hand gestures. It turns out to be a false alarm. The oncoming lights are actually police helicopters that have come to search the area. Pye and Myles note that Spielberg's story is full of cheating: "A police helicopter is silent until it lands so that we may momentarily think it is a UFO."[24] The actions of the helicopters, with their whirling blades kicking up a windstorm, appear more ominous and threatening than the alien craft the night before. Everyone runs for cover to escape this intrusion by the authorities. Spielberg delights in making authority figures wear black hats, which is about as close as he comes to making an antiestablishment statement (he is after all a new generation filmmaker who grew up during the turmoil of the sixties; but, of the movie brats, only Francis Ford Coppola has ventured major political comment with films like *You're a Big Boy Now, The Conversation,* and *Apocalypse Now*).[25]

The action cuts to the international scene, where cartographer Laughlin, Lacombe, and other members of the team are investigating pulses received from outer space. Williams's five notes register when the pulses are converted by computers into numbers, generating musical tones. The numbers are recognized by Laughlin as map coordinates. Hence the opening scene (added later) explains why a cartographer, hired as a translator, is on hand to recognize this important data.

It is no secret that Spielberg likes to "test" his films in the editing process to uncover their flaws and better pace the action. The result can sometimes appear as a manufactured scenario that is technically superior but dramatically inferior, a charge often leveled at Spielberg. Such scenes, however, reveal Spielberg's fascination with and respect for science. He loves machines and surrounds his scientists with them. He also uses technical jargon to add a touch of realism in the tradition of Kubrick's *2001*.

In an adolescently humourous scene, some of the scientists break into the supervisor's office to retrieve a globe of the earth (they roll it down the hallway like a bunch of kids with a beach ball). They need it to pinpoint the location designated by the map coordinates; it is somewhere in the state of Wyoming.

The scene cuts to Jillian's secluded house where Barry is playing the five-note sequence on his toy xylophone. Jillian is outside hanging clothes when lights appear in a sky that is clouding over. She runs inside, bolting all doors and windows. The light attempts to enter through the fireplace, but Jillian is quick to shut the flue. The house is under siege. The stove begins to glow bright red and the vacuum cleaner chases them around the living room. In a moment of silence, Jillian watches the screws from the floor furnace vent undo themselves. The aliens are trying to get in from under the house. She reacts by throwing a rug over the vent. Preoccupied in keeping the aliens at bay, Jillian loses sight of Barry, who is trying to get out of the house through the back door. He wants to play with the aliens. Apparently he is not afraid. A terrified Jillian runs into the kitchen to save her son. He is halfway out the door when she grabs him, but the force on the other side is too great. Barry is pulled through the door and disappears. Jillian runs out of the house, only to see the alien craft dance through the clouds and disappear. Pye and Myles note of this scene that "the sense of menace within the home parallels Hitchcock's *The Birds*."[26]

Spielberg takes us to the site of Devil's Tower, the exact location the map coordinates have indicated. The military has been called in to clear the area. This is done by announcing a fake train derailment that has supposedly released lethal gas into the atmosphere. Preparations are underway to move the scientific team and all their instruments to the top of Devil's Tower. They feel that a meeting with the aliens will take place. A team of men and women is also being readied, volunteers ready to go with the aliens if the chance arises. Spielberg creates a number of harried scenes for this sequence, in order to move the narrative quickly along.

Spielberg then cuts to the Neary household, where things are beginning to fall apart. The children are not sure what to make of Dad, who appears "different." At the dinner table one night, Roy begins building a mountainlike structure out of his mashed potatoes, sculpting it with his dinner fork. Spielberg enjoys the subtle interplay of references to earlier sci-fi films. Clearly, Dad has been changed in some way leaving the family to speculate the worst—is he an alien as depicted in *The Invasion of the Body Snatchers* or a possessed human working for the aliens? His children look puzzled and upset, but Roy tries to calm them by explaining that he is still "Daddy." His wife is more skeptical, however, seeing it as a weird obsession that is scaring her half to death. Finally, she can take no more. She packs up the kids one morning and drives off to her sister's, leaving Roy (who jumps on the hood of the car to reason with her) sitting in the driveway surrounded by a collection of gawking neighbors.

In the lonely days that follow, Roy becomes hermitlike trying to make sense out of his experience. He has been implanted with an image of a mountainlike structure. But what is it? What does it mean? Roy begins to sculpt the structure in the den atop the train layout seen earlier in the film. Spielberg delights in contrasting the banality of suburban life with a once healthy middle-class male gone mad. It not only takes the heavy edge off the drama, but serves to give the film a charm and sense of wonder that would otherwise have been lost. In one scene, Roy stares out his sliding glass doors at all his middle-class neighbors performing their middle-class activities: cutting grass, barbecuing, watering the lawn. Spielberg reveals that Roy's obsession is too great to reenter that middle-class reality when he has him close the drapes. He is trapped, and his only way out is to discover the meaning of the image he has been sculpting.

Roy is hard at work shaping the image in his mind while the television behind him broadcasts news coverage of evacuation of the Devil's Tower area as a result of the industrial "accident." In a contrived suspense-building scene, Neary finally notices the news, seeing Devil's Tower for the first time. Immediately he knows what his symbolic icon means. He compares the television image to his own sculpture. He appears pleased that his sculpture comes so close in detail to the actual Devil's Tower (much later in the film, Roy quips to another enlightened individual that he would have known what was on the other side of Devil's Tower if he had sculpted the structure). A parallel scene shows that Jillian also has the implanted vision of the mountainlike structure. Sketches of the image hang all about her house. She also sees the television report and recognizes Devil's Tower as the image in her mind. Although their journeys to Wyoming begin separately, Roy and Jillian eventually find each other at the train depot.

It is important to the plot that Roy and Jillian share experiences that make them different and isolate them from others—in Roy's case, even from his wife and children. They and the other characters (usually unnamed) who have encounters develop a need to seek out the UFOs, even though they are discouraged and eventually forcibly prevented from doing so by the military.

Lacombe is the link among the victims of these encounters, the military, who try to stage a massive cover-up of the events, the scientific community, and the alien beings themselves. His interest appears to be in linguistic communication; at one point, he is seen at an international conference lecturing on language and the use of sign language. In the final climactic meeting with an alien being, Lacombe communicates through hand signals and musical tones.

The casting of François Truffaut, French filmmaker and critic, in the part of Lacombe was extremely appropriate, as Annette Insdorf points out:

> The result of this casting is that Spielberg's science-fiction extravaganza is enriched by the theme of language on both a personal and cosmic scale. As Lacombe, Truffaut uses an interpreter since he speaks mostly French; this limitation in communicating is counterpointed by his ability to "speak" with the creature who emerges from the spaceship. At the beginning of *Close Encounters*, Lacombe is first to realize that music is one of their means of communication . . . and, at the

film's climax, he embarks upon the first exchange with the aliens through hand signals (like a teacher of the deaf) and an infectious smile.[27]

Indeed, Truffaut's smile is luminous. So is Barry's. Spielberg used special lighting techniques to enhance this "magical," "starlike" quality. Both Barry and Lacombe represent purity—Barry, childlike innocence, and Lacombe, the purity of science. The military, on the other hand, are portrayed as corrupt. They lie to people who come to them with UFO reports in order to cover up their own attempts to make contact with the aliens.

In spite of the military's efforts, the people who have reported encounters, including Roy Neary and Jillian Guiler, make their way to the site. Roy is so affected by his encounter that once at Devil's Tower he is compelled to go away with the creatures. He will never be the same again—just as many in real life who have reported encounters with alien beings have not been able to assimilate their experiences without psychic pain.

After attempts by authorities to stop them, Roy, Jillian, and one other persistent man make their way up Devil's Tower. The commander, who has been given the task of removing all civilians from the mountain, issues an order to spray EZ-4, a chemical that induces sleep. The trio spot the spraying helicopters and attempt to escape their path. The man with Roy and Jillian catches a dose of EZ-4, falls to the ground, and goes to sleep. This sequence is a homage, as critics like *Time* reviewer Frank Rich have observed, to other films Spielberg has admired: "Roy Neary (Dreyfuss) is a . . . kind of man-in-the-middle played by Cary Grant and James Stewart in films like *North by Northwest* and *Vertigo*."[28]

Roy and Jillian finally make it to Box Canyon, on the other side of Devil's Tower. In front of them lies what looks like a portable air field. At the base of the plateau, an array of technicians, machines, and instruments is assembled to record the alien encounter. A large scoreboardlike sign faces the runway. Connected to an electronic organ, it displays musical tones in specific colors. Roy and Jillian watch the action from their protected perch on the mountainside.

Finally, the moment everyone is waiting for arrives. Sensors pick up alien craft in the area, and everyone darts to his respective position as if it had been rehearsed a hundred times before. The same alien spaceships Roy and Jillian spotted on that lonely roadside in Muncie, including the tiny red craft bringing up the rear, fly past them again. The alien craft hover on the runway facing the technicians, who initiate communication by playing the tones. After a moment of silence, the spaceships respond with similar tones, then quickly fly off. What comes next is not certain. Spielberg lets the audience catch its breath for only a moment before clouds boil up over Devil's Tower. Finally, a huge mothership comes into view and descends toward the runway.

Roy and Jillian look in awe as the chandelierlike ship slowly moves over the peak of Devil's Tower. It is the Magic Kingdom come to life. Slowly it positions itself above the scientists. In grand style, the superstructure of brilliant light and sparkling crystal slowly turns upside down before coming to rest just above ground on the runway.

The wondrous grand design of the universe is coming together for earthlings to see. Wanting us to bathe in this "encounter of the third kind," Spielberg creates a uniquely rich scene that is unparalleled in film history—scientists scramble, photo-motion cameras whiz, a barrage of scientific instruments processes a trillion bits of data. As before, the scientists begin communication through the electronic organ and light display by playing the five-note theme over and over. Eventually, the mother ship responds. After a brief exchange of communication, someone wants to know if the lesson is being recorded. "It's the first day of school, fellas," one scientist blurts out as another punches the record button on a multitrack recorder. As the musical revue intensifies, it becomes reminiscent of the dueling banjos sequence in *Deliverance* (1972). The interchange becomes so intense that a pane of glass in one of the observation towers shatters.

Once these formalities are over, the mother ship whines and the bottom hatch lowers to the ground. An intense, blinding light sprays out of the opening. The scientists pull back, not knowing what to expect, yet sensing in a strange, intuitive way what is to come. This scene exemplifies one of Spielberg's most interesting approaches to film action—that he usually plays it for suspense. He has been criticized for this, however.

The first beings to march out of the alien spaceship are human—various military personnel and civilians who have been abducted by the aliens in the past. A table with photos of missing persons has been preassembled and placed in position. As the humans march out of the mothership, they give their name, rank, and serial number, at which their pictures are crossed out. Barry also comes strolling out—to Jillian's surprise and delight.

By this time, Roy has left the protected enclave on the cliff and joined the activity center stage. Meanwhile, a team of men and women have assembled to go with the aliens. Jillian decides to stay behind, probably because of her commitment to her young son, although this is never explicitly stated. Roy joins this group of space travelers, suiting up in a bright orange outfit to leave Earth.

While these adventurers stand in front of the beaming white light, a small group of aliens descends from the opening, surrounding Roy as if he were a specially invited guest. According to Balaban, Spielberg was particularly careful with the extraterrestrials' overall "look."[29] For example, one proposal had the children wearing headpieces resembling fetuses when they disembark from the mothership; these headpieces were redesigned several times before Spielberg was satisfied. In addition, an original skating idea was dropped in favor of having the children dance as they descend to greet the humans. It was suggested that some could fly out of the hatch on wires, recalling Disney's *Peter Pan* complete with Tinker Bell–type fairies.

In the final version, however, the extraterrestrials merely walk out of the hatch in a childlike way and greet Roy. Spielberg is careful to let us see them only from the rear and not their faces. Apparently he was not happy with the final head-pieces, nor was he enthusiastic about having them fly out of the spaceship Disney-style. After the aliens lead Roy into the spaceship, the adult extraterrestrial (Crawley notes that Spielberg named him Puck) descends from the hatch ramp to greet his earthly hosts. An extremely bright, diffuse light hides most of its features, but the viewer is able to tell that it is thin, slender, and frail.[30] It was crucial that the audience accept the creature as something warm and wondrous, which was the feeling Spielberg wanted from the film as a whole—very gentle, almost an embrace.[31] For this effect Spielberg felt it was necessary to show the alien in detail. Pye and Myles suggest, "there is a reason for showing the alien's face . . . the film subverts the familiar paranoia of science fiction made during the Cold War. The alien must be clearly seen in order to banish fear."[32]

For this sensational scene, Spielberg used very strong back-lighting to produce a mystical sense of a heavenly appearance: the alien opens its arms in a prayerful, peace-loving way. Reaction shots of the scientists, now wearing sunglasses to protect their eyes against the radiant light, reveal them fixed and rigid, standing in awe as they witness this won-drous event. In a touching scene played against Williams's five-note melody, Lacombe handsignals the alien with a greeting and the alien responds with a smile. Balaban notes this moment in a discussion of the film's preview.

> I watch the movie in a daze. . . . The Mothership I had pictured was a very dark hulk with some flashing lights, and what I am looking at is a spectacular city of lights. Things that I pretend-ed to be looking at for months in Mobile are flashing by for real, this time, and I can't get over the fact that it really works. All those "look to the left and be surprised"'s are paying off. . . . And when Truffaut finally does his hand signals to Carlo Ram-baldi's lone figure, I can hear sniffling all around us.[33]

When the alien returns to the mothership, the hatch closes, the spaceship begins to lift off the runway, and the musical score swells. Jillian looks on while her son, Barry, waves his arm and utters a touching "Goodbye, goodbye." All of this could have easily collapsed into pure camp except for Spielberg's meticulous preparation, which established this long sequence as something magnificent, wondrous, and essential to human understanding in the universe. The use of music, light, and realistic visual effects made this scene so persuasive that credibility was maintained, if just barely—even during the orchestrated "When You Wish upon A Star" theme added in the special edition. In the first version, Spielberg had planned to use original music by Ukelele Ike, but he later explained to Balaban and others that he got "a lot of unfavorable comments about the song at the preview of the film in Dallas" and decided to cut it for this reason.[34]

DIFFERENCES IN THE TWO VERSIONS

When *Close Encounters* was released, Spielberg hinted that he had been working on a sequel but refused to give any details of the story or its characters. Many theorized that it might be Roy Neary's adventure with the aliens as they circled the universe visiting other alien civilizations. Others predicted that it might be the story of Roy Neary after he was returned to Earth by the alien.[35] But Spielberg remained silent. The success of the original prompted Columbia pictures to press him for a sequel. According to Tony Crawley, Spielberg stated he was writing the sequel in early 1978 and that production would begin by that summer. However, it was not until 1979 that Spielberg wrote a story for the sequel (entitled "Night Skies"), turning it over to writer-director John Sayles (*Return of the Secaucus Seven*, 1978) for the screenplay. At this time, Spielberg also mentioned he would only produce, not direct (leaving that job up to Ron Cobb, a good friend of John Milius).[36]

When the "Night Skies" project fell through, Spielberg suggested restructuring *Close Encounters* into a special edition and the studio agreed. As Spielberg recalls: "My attitude is very simply that the *Special Edition* would have been the first film had I two more months. I didn't have the time and so, as a result, the entire second act of the first film is for me very unsatisfying. Specifically, the pacing between Richard's story and the François Truffaut story, and the correlation, symbolically, that one has toward the other is much more deliberate in the Special Edition than it is in the original version."[37]

The two major sequences filmed for the special edition show the international team of scientists investigating a ghost ship in the Gobi desert and Roy Neary venturing inside the alien spaceship. Minor additions included some footage of Truffaut in India and the passage of a large shadow over the land.[38] The other changes in the film are not so noticeable because Spielberg mainly reedited the film, deleting some scenes to propel the action, and, in some cases, using a different take of a scene than was used in the original.[39] The deletions include: the sequence in which Roy is frantically running around his front yard collecting bushes and dirt to build his miniature Devil's Tower; Roy working at his job; a UFO-watcher on Crescendo Summit exclaiming, "They can fly rings around the moon, but we're years ahead of them on the highway"; and military guards attempting to stop Roy and Jillian on Devil's Tower.[40]

CRITICISM

The film is not without its faults. As Pye and Myles note, a mystical interpretation of the story "goes for nothing when it is intercut with the literal presentation of the alien race." "The first alien to leave the ship is a shadow, spreading its arms in apparent benediction. . . . [This image] is spoiled by sledge-hammer cutting to reaction shots that tell us to feel wonder, by the over-literal score of John Williams, and by an insistence on taking us close to the alien so that the mystery dissipates in simple appreciation of technical skill."[41]

The episodic nature of *Close Encounters* barely leaves viewers time to catch their breath before the spectacular ending. Sequences rocket along until the magic at Devil's Tower begins. Although faulted for putting technical virtuosity ahead of characterization (the episodic nature of the film also detracts from the characterizations), Spielberg was only seeking to present "everyman" and "everywoman."

A major criticism of the special edition was that it was not so special. Spielberg was accused of sloppily throwing in the spectacular Gobi desert sequence.[42] In the effort to quicken the pace, the suburban "everydayness" of the Neary family is lost. As a result, Roy "goes mad" much more quickly in the new version. As for the sequence where Roy enters the spaceship, Crawley disappointingly notes: "All great expectations disappeared as Dreyfuss entered the hatchway of the Mother Ship—and very little else happened at all. Some machinery lowered and moved around him, cueing the director to hit the button and turn on his latest Duracell illuminations. And that was all. Spielberg never allowed more views of the ETs, never mind closer views of the inner workings, size or scope of the ship. Th-th-that's all folks! Up, up and away!"[43]

SPIELBERG'S CLOSE ENCOUNTER

This was the first film in which Spielberg not only directed, but also conceived, wrote the original story, and participated in designing the special effects. In classic Spielbergian tradition, the film is a running tribute to film history, paying homage to *The Birds* (1963), *North by Northwest* (1959), *Pinocchio* (1940), *Bambi* (1942), *Fantasia* (1940), and *Invaders from Mars* (1953). According to Pye and Myles, *Close Encounters* is "the ultimate statement about suburbia, about the death of the ideology that killed the old system of Hollywood. It is appropriate that the diagnosis should be made by one of the children of Hollywood, for *Close Encounters* ends with the millennium, and Spielberg is the prophet."[44]

At one point during the filming, several people thought they spotted a real UFO in the sky above the Mobile hangar housing the Box Canyon set.[45] Had the UFO been real (it turned out to be a weather balloon), it would have been the perfect experience for Spielberg—bridging the fantasy of film and the reality of UFOs. It would have been Walt Disney's Magic Kingdom brought to life.

Spielberg's prophetic vision of UFOs and alien beings is unique, considering the Cold War science-fiction films of the 1950s and 1960s that depicted extraterrestrials as monsters bent on destroying Earth and the human race. By contrast, Spielberg's aliens are quite friendly (although cautious) and want to communicate with us. They even want a legitimate cultural exchange program. But Spielberg keeps his vision hidden until the end; for most of the film he appears to support the old clichés: Barry is abducted, and Roy and Jillian are driven close to insanity in their quest to unravel the mysteries implanted in their minds. "Can we really trust them?" is a question Spielberg keeps asking until everything converges in a joyous and wondrous event similar to the mystical coming of the Star Child in *2001: A Space Odyssey*. Spielberg's unique, spiritual vision of life from other worlds is best described by Pauline Kael in the *New Yorker:* "God is up there in a crystal-chandelier spaceship and He likes us."[46]

5 / *Animal House*
Goes to War: *1941*

Spielberg's next film, *1941*, is in the comedy-action genre and, indeed, neither the comedy nor the action ever stops. A combination of *It's a Mad Mad Mad Mad World* (1963) and *The Longest Day* (1962), the film relates the comic story of an attempted invasion by a Japanese fleet off the California coastline during World War II. Spielberg obviously did not learn from Stanley Kramer's *Mad Mad World*, which contains numerous subplots, that bigger does not necessarily mean better. As Spielberg himself comments, *1941* has at least "seven simultaneous plot lines" and succeeds mainly in exhausting and bewildering the viewer. Although the zany film may be, as Coursodon and Sâuvage comment, a failure as a comedy, it is also "a highly original *directorial* experiment."[1]

A précis of the story follows. Boy (Bobby Di Cicco) meets girl (Dianne Kay). Boy wants to take girl to a USO dance even though he is not in uniform. Girl's father (Ned Beatty) prepares for invasion. Meanwhile, a Japanese submarine is hovering off the California coast, preparing to invade an amusement park, while an American general (marvelously played by Robert Stack) watches his favorite film—*Dumbo*—at a theater. To save the day, Wild Bill Kelso (John Belushi) roars up on his motorcycle, commandeers a fighter bomber, and creates havoc in the streets, while the general's aide (Tim Matheson) tries to seduce the general's secretary (Nancy Allen) in a runaway airplane. These plot lines eventually work their way toward a spectacular grand finale in which a full-sized house, rigged by special effects wizard A. D. Flowers, crashes from the top of a cliff to the coastline below.

The script for *1941* was written by Robert Zemeckis and

Bob Gale for a USC film class taught by John Milius.[2] Milius had encouraged them to develop the script which he found outrageously funny. He attempted to secure financing for the script, which was formerly called "Hollywood '41" and later "The Rising Sun," but without success.[3] Eventually, Milius gave the project to Spielberg (who was in preproduction with *Close Encounters*) and turned his attention to a "personal" film about a group of surfers entitled *Big Wednesday* (1978).[4] Bob Balaban notes that in 1976, Zemeckis and Gale went to Mobile, where Spielberg was filming *Close Encounters*.[5] During their eight-week stay, Spielberg directed *Close Encounters* by day, while by night the three screened old war films and worked on the screenplay for *1941*. Says Spielberg, "I was being dragged helplessly through the streets by this crazo [*sic*] script."[6] Spielberg tackled the project head-on despite his doubts. It was produced through Milius's A-Team Productions.

With *Close Encounters* wrapped up, Spielberg immediately began work on *1941*. Says Spielberg: "All of the big action set pieces were pre-planned, as they have been in every movie that I've done. The dogfight over Hollywood Blvd. (which creates the "invisible" air raid), the Japanese assault on Ocean Park in Santa Monica—set pieces like that were prearranged through hundreds of sketches done by George Jensen. . . . We sat down six months before even the first miniature was built and sketched together. We did the storyboards for the entire movie. . . . Everything was pre-planned in the greatest detail."[7]

Next, Gregory Jein began working on the miniatures with his crew of forty model builders. Spielberg claims *1941* has "the best miniature work since that of the Lydecker brothers in the forties and fifties."[8] Jein's crew produced highly detailed models, which William Fraker, Spielberg's cinematographer for the film, found "so beautiful."[9] Fraker also notes that while live action is usually photographed first and later matched to the miniatures, this was not the case with *1941*,

since Fraker began filming the miniatures first.[10] This procedure required that explicit notes be taken on the lighting of
the miniatures, which were then matched to the live action
sequences filmed six months later.

Fraker conducted numerous filter tests, hoping to find the
right "look" before production began, but he was not satisfied
with the results. He eventually used a number two fog filter
to achieve the forties period look both he and Spielberg wanted.[11] This particular filter blended the hard lines created by
focused spotlights (which produce a "hard" light source)
while the practical lights (lights actually seen in the shot)
flared out, producing a pleasing glow around them.

Fraker also decided to photograph the miniatures in a
smoke-filled room because he said it gave them "a feeling of
texture on the screen. . . . Consequently we had to continue
that later on with the actual photography. As a result, almost
every shot has smoke in it."[12] The main advantage of filming
miniatures through a smoke-filled atmosphere, as evidenced
in Ridley Scott's *Alien* (1979) and *Blade Runner* (1981), is that
it increases the apparent atmospheric distance between the
camera and the miniature itself. It creates such a realistic image that viewers are forced to look very closely to determine
that what they are viewing is indeed a miniature.

The Louma crane, best described as a camera hung on the
end of a sound boom, was developed in France. Spielberg said
he saw the effect of the Louma crane on a videotape commercial being circulated to demonstrate its versatility.[13] He eventually got to see the device perform firsthand in Deauville,
France, in 1977, and decided to use it only for "mock-up shots
simulating flight and for the big dance number in the middle
of the picture."[14] The Louma crane (previously used for several shots on the James Bond film *Moonraker* [1979] and
Superman [1978] proved so versatile that it became Spielberg's "A" camera for filming live-action sequences and for
numerous shots of the miniatures. Spielberg writes, "I'm very
demanding when it comes to filling the frame and composing

it nicely and found that, with the 15-foot arm on the LOUMA Crane, I could fish for the right shot by looking at the monitor and I could get just the shot I wanted, as opposed to getting on the Fisher dolly and having them push me in two feet and crab to the right a foot and go up on the [boom] arm a couple of inches."[15]

To simulate aircraft movement in flight, Spielberg's production team built a gimbal (at a cost of thirty-five thousand dollars) to maneuver the Beechcraft and P-40 aircraft: "There is a whole sequence that takes place in the Beechcraft where Tim Matheson [the general's aide] and Nancy Allen [the general's secretary] are fornicating at 10,000 feet."[16] Both aircraft were reconstructed on sound stages and attached to the gimbal when aircraft movement was needed, but Spielberg felt the gimbal's movement was inadequate for simulated airplane movement. Several times, he resorted to the Louma crane to produce the fluid movements he felt best represented an airplane in flight.

1941 was Spielberg's first film shot almost exclusively within the confines of Hollywood's sound stages. Even the submarine shots off the coast of California were filmed in a giant swimming pool on stage 30 at MGM, where Esther Williams had performed her most graceful underwater scenes in front of the cameras for *Bathing Beauty* (1944).[17] This was a new experience for Spielberg, who usually shot his feature films entirely on location, either inland (*Duel* and *Sugarland Express*) or on the real waters of the Atlantic Ocean (*Jaws*), and who had built his own "studio" on location in Alabama (*Close Encounters of the Third Kind*).

WAR IS "HELL"-ARIOUS

Although it could justifiably be billed as an antiwar movie, Spielberg is quoted as saying adamantly, "'1941' is a comedy not a war picture."[18] It would be Spielberg's first extended venture into comedy, a genre that is probably the hardest to execute in the cinema. Gerald Mast, in his book *The Comic Mind*, asserts:

> Perhaps the only term for describing the successful marriage between comic intention and execution is one of the key concepts of the Renaissance—*sprezzatura*. . . . In general, the impression of *sprezzatura* is a matter of rhythm and emphasis—when to cut and when not to cut, what to emphasize and what to gloss over . . . when to use the close-up to reveal a human reaction or concrete detail, when to stay further away to allow the viewer to infer it; how long to remain with that close-up; what kinds of business are genuinely funny, what angle and distance illuminate that humor; when to cut quickly away from a facial reaction, a piece of business or a line and when to prolong the shot.[19]

It was not surprising that Spielberg had second thoughts about the project. Crawley notes that Spielberg was "still iffy" before production began,[20] and Chris Hodenfield, in a *Rolling Stone* interview with Spielberg, comments that "he left his strong suit—the art of creating suspense—hanging in the closet."[21] Spielberg, like John Ford,[22] used comic touches in his earlier films, but their overall intention was not comic. Crawley even speculates that Milius backed out of directing *1941* because he, like Spielberg, knew nothing about making a comedy.[23]

To compensate for his lack of experience, Spielberg decided to rely heavily on casting comedians, since he felt they would do "some funny things."[24] "But trying to figure out what's funny and what isn't is like trying to predict earthquakes in California."[25] This was probably Spielberg's first mistake, as Mast notes: "A film . . . is truly funny when the audience is not conscious that it intends to be funny. As soon as one becomes aware of artifice and fakery (not the kind that functions as an integral part of the comic climate), comedy disintegrates into banal and obnoxious posturing. Although intellectual detachment is crucially related to the experience of successful comedy, when the detachment becomes so great that the mind is no longer amused and engaged but notes the gap between intention and accomplishment, concept and execution, the comedy fails to amuse and entertain."[26]

Spielberg's use of Dan Aykroyd and John Belushi, both graduates of NBC's "Saturday Night Live" television show, revealed his intention to make the film funny. These dons of improvisational comedy represent the new wave of seventies comics, who, along with Steve Martin and Chevy Chase, had proven popular with the college crowd and with younger audiences. Their comic personas are hybrids of the wacky characters featured on Rowan and Martin's "Laugh-In" comedy television series of the late sixties crossed with the pointedly outrageous and cynical machinations of Lenny Bruce in the fifties. They do not hesitate to resort to low comedy (like Mel Brooks's *Blazing Saddles*, 1974) even to the point of grossness seen in several tasteless skits produced on "Saturday Night Live." Those viewers who did not find Belushi or Aykroyd amusing "are really saying that their attempts to be funny are obvious and hence do not succeed at making comic life out of contrived business."[27] The casting of Aykroyd and Belushi destroyed the possibility of perceiving the film in any way except as wacky comedy (Spielberg himself likened the film to the early forties comedy *Hellzapoppin* [1941]). Aykroyd did his usual fast-talking, shtick routine while Belushi's character was a modified version of the fat, slobbering Bluto from *National Lampoon's Animal House* (1978).

Crawley notes that it was Zemeckis and Gale's style to pack their script with "loons and idiots": "That was the trouble with '78. Loons were in. The *National Lampoon's Animal House* syndrome had begun. It is still around, alas, with the *Porky's* films. Just why Steven Spielberg felt he had to join in with such unruly messes is one, the only, aberration in his career to date."[28]

The film's failure as a comedy is unique because all the elements of comic persuasion seem to be present: contemporary comedians (John Belushi and Dan Aykroyd), great character actors (Warren Oates, Robert Stack, Slim Pickens, Christopher Lee, and Toshiro Mifune), fantastic sets and convincing miniatures, clever comic bits, and innovative sight gags. Even Chuck Jones, the cartoon animator behind Road Runner and Bugs Bunny, was consulted in the early stages of production.[29] In addition, the film employs at least five of eight comic plots described by Mast: (1) new comedy, where boy (Bobby Di Cicco) meets girl (Dianne Kay), boy loses girl, boy gets girl; (2) intentional parody or burlesque of another film (Spielberg's opening scene in *1941* parodies the opening scene of *Jaws*); (3) accelerated reductio ad absurdum, where a simple human mistake or social question is magnified, thereby reducing the action to chaos and the social question to absurdity; (4) "riffing" or "goofing," defined as the "improvised and anomalous gaggery" evident in many of Chaplin's Keystones because it was one of two major Mack Sennett structures (the other being parody), which involved initiating a particular situation and running a series of gags around it; (5) subtle reductio ad absurdum, described as an "investigation of the workings of a particular society, comparing the responses of one social group or class with those of another, contrasting people's different responses to the same stimuli and similar responses to different stimuli. Such plots are usually multi-leveled, containing two, three, or even more parallel lines of action."[30]

What went wrong? Chris Hodenfield notes that, despite the use of classic plots, traditional comic elements are missing:

> The slow burn, the double take, the dreadful anticipation, the witty rejoinder—were abandoned for the continuous slam-bang. For instance, if you knew beforehand that a paint factory was waiting behind closed doors, and that a careening army tank was heading straight for it, well, you'd be waiting. As it stands, the viewer is suddenly aware that a paint factory has materialized and this army tank is crashing through it. Or, in a café, a man's face pitching toward a counter suddenly meets a birthday cake. The mind registers these various happenings moments after the eye perceives them.[31]

Spielberg became so worried that the film contained "holes" where laughs should be heard, he trimmed it back several more minutes after the Denver and Dallas test previews.[32] Hodenfield suggests that Spielberg "might have cut too close to the bone" in trimming the film at the expense of fuller development of subplots and characters, leaving behind nothing more than a film "full of strangers."[33] No sooner is the audience introduced to one set of characters than the next set appears. Even comic actor Dan Aykroyd comments: "There were so many elements that had to be chopped out because the movie was so big, and [Spielberg] had to get it down to a manageable time."[34] Although Spielberg tried to correct the overall "conceptual disasters" of *1941*, he could not salvage the entire film.[35] He hoped that John Williams's musical score would help, but the thunderous music only added to the zany proportions of a wacky film comedy out of control. "Johnny's been overwriting [his score] over my overdirection over Zemeckis and Gale's overwritten script," Spielberg said.[36] The basic problem with the film was that it was in incredibly bad taste, and each overexaggerated new element made the situation worse. The difference from *Animal House* is that the very title *1941* still depresses many Americans—even the idea of a potential enemy invasion is not funny and cannot be made so by Keystone Cops slapstick.

Because it is such a failure, a close look at the entire movie is not necessary; nevertheless, certain scenes are worth noting, for they show the "technical virtuosity" for which Spielberg is known. For example, the USO dance scene contains frenzied kinetic action that never stops from the moment the characters begin to dance until the fight stops. Spielberg's choreography of this scene, fluidly filmed by veteran cinematographer William Fraker, stands up to the best Busby Berkeley or Fred Astaire–Ginger Rogers musicals of the thirties. The scene, interspersed with a number of slapstick sight gags, employed the use of an old dance rig that had originally helped Fred Astaire to dance on walls and ceilings in MGM's *Royal Wedding* (1951).[37]

The shots of Wild Bill Kelso's airplane flying through the streets of Los Angeles set a new standard in miniature photography. Jein's set was highly detailed, containing thousands of small lights (all the shots of the miniature were at night) to illuminate windows, miniature car headlights, lamp poles, and Christmas bulbs strung across the miniature boulevard. When Kelso finally reaches the outskirts of the city after downing a plane he believed to be a Japanese fighter (it actually contains the general's aide and secretary), he sees the commotion below and surmises the Japanese have landed. Flying low between the tall buildings of the city, he conducts a one-man assault, which further escalates the havoc below. The plane, rigged on wires, was flown through the streets of the miniature set and photographed using the Louma crane, which could photograph objects as close as one-and-a-half inches off the floor. Eventually Kelso's bomber crashes, but he quickly jumps out to aid his tank commander (Dan Aykroyd). The streets and surrounding buildings are slowly destroyed as pandemonium continues. The USO club, destroyed on the inside by the fight at the beginning of the film, is further demolished on the outside by gun and tank fire. Vehicles, strewn everywhere, are further destroyed by Aykroyd's tank, which runs over them in a manic fury.

In another scene, the Japanese, positioned for attack in their submarine, torpedo the amusement park, also a miniature. Two natives stand lookout atop the ferris wheel, which is located close to a pier that juts out into the Pacific. One lookout (Eddie Deezen, who plays the part in the style of ventriloquist Edgar Bergen), has a "dummy" at his side, which further reduces the film to lunacy. Finally, a torpedo makes a direct hit on the ferris wheel, causing it to fall off its supports, and roll down the pier and into the ocean.

Other comic bits include a motorcycle chase, Aykroyd's tank crashing through a paint factory, and the locals' attempt at self-annihilation (Ned Beatty blows a hole through his own house with an artillery shell).

Spielberg's techniques for the film are his standard quick

cutting between subplots and speeding up the dialogue, but this does not keep the segments from appearing overdone. Where Spielberg succeeds, as Coursodon notes, is in his genius for holding the parts together until the final scene, where Beatty's house, now almost destroyed, slides off the cliff to the rocks below. At least he delivers a cohesive whole, regardless of how flawed the action or idiotic the premise.

6 / The Adventures of Indiana Jones

Spielberg's collaboration with George Lucas put his directorial career back on track in 1981 with the highly successful, under budget, and ahead of schedule *Raiders of the Lost Ark*. Curiously enough, the 1984 sequel, or "prequel," as it is billed, *Indiana Jones and the Temple of Doom*, slightly tarnished Spielberg's reputation because of its controversial violence. The intense outcry about its suitability for the very young (who flocked to see it), led to the creation by fall 1984 of a new motion picture rating code called PG-13 (Parental guidance suggested for children under 13). To his credit, Spielberg was in the vanguard of the movement, stating publicly that he would not let a ten-year-old see *Temple of Doom*. He later commented that "the responsibility to the children of this country is worth any loss at the box office."[1]

RAIDERS OF THE LOST ARK

Raiders, whose plot and hero are based on the serials that were popular Saturday matinee fare with young movie audiences in the thirties and forties, belongs solely in the action genre. Directed by Spielberg, the script by Lawrence Kasdan (who was recommended to George Lucas by Spielberg) takes its hero, archaeologist Indiana Jones, through a series of fast-paced adventures. He tries to retrieve the "Lost Ark of the Covenant" from headhunters, snakepits, and Nazi villains in a chase that takes him literally around the world.[2]

To escape his depression in the months that followed *1941*'s release, Spielberg threw himself into the *Raiders* project.

Three men—Spielberg, Lucas, and Kasdan—began working on the adventures of Lucas's archaeologist playboy. Lucas and Spielberg had differing ideas on the "look" of the film. Pollock notes: "Spielberg wanted *Raiders* to be the movie equivalent of a ride at Disneyland, inexpensive but believable. Lucas wanted it to remain true to the 1930s serials, with gruff dialogue, plenty of action, and cheap sets. As with *Star Wars*, Lucas insisted that *Raiders* be played straight—the characters and situations were not to be mocked. The audience had to laugh with the picture, not at it."[3]

Lucas gave Spielberg a very specific formula to follow: the screenplay was divided into sixty scenes, each two pages long, and it outlined the six dramatic situations that Indiana would find himself in. Lucas comments, "It's a serialesque movie. . . . It's also basically an action piece. We want to keep things interspaced and at the same time build tension."[4] Building tension was Spielberg's specialty, considering his previous action-thriller films *Duel* and *Jaws*. Since the opening sequence in *Raiders* would make or break the film, Lucas wanted something special. It was Spielberg who designed the opening sequence, which climaxes with Indy narrowly escaping death from a huge tumbling boulder after he has pilfered a sacred Peruvian artifact from a hidden temple. The scene immediately establishes the hang-on-to-your-seats feeling that sets the tone and pace for the rest of the film.

Raiders, like *1941*, was another departure from Spielberg's own style of filmmaking. After *Jaws* was released, Richard Combs asked Spielberg if he saw a similarity among his films or a stylistic continuity. Spielberg replied that he sensed similarities between *Duel* and *Jaws* and a "similarity between *The Sugarland Express* and a film I'm about to begin" (presumably Spielberg was referring either to *1941* or to *Continental Divide* [1981], which he was originally scheduled to direct, but never did). "But as far as style within a body of work is concerned, I'm a little too subjective to have feelings about that. . . . I don't think I've made enough films to do that yet, and most of my films haven't been as personal as I think I am to myself."[5] Actually, the unique lighting style Spielberg developed for *Close Encounters* became the trademark of his subsequent "personal" films such as *E.T.: The Extra-Terrestrial*, *Poltergeist*, and his "Kick the Can" segment in *Twilight Zone: The Movie*. (This style is present in *1941*, but was virtually overwhelmed by the film's overworked slapstick.)

But the emerging visual style of Spielberg's work—diffused images that are strongly backlit and countered with a weak fill light—would not fit the *Raiders* scenario as Lucas envisioned it. It was to be shot straightforward, without diffusion photography or Spielberg's special lighting techniques.[6] In Lucas's mind, the overall look for the film was to be akin to the "Adventure Theater" television shows he had watched in his youth. The character of Indiana (or Indy, as his friends refer to him) was envisioned by Lucas as a disheveled playboy similar to Humphrey Bogart in *The Treasure of the Sierra Madre* (1948). Harrison Ford, who was chosen for the part, offered this sober, candid description of the character: "He's a grave robber!"[7] There were many similarities between Indiana Jones and the Han Solo character that Ford had played in *Star Wars*. Both were rebels, but Lucas wanted Indy to have some morals. He was to be the traditional "white-hatted" protagonist facing all odds against "black-hooded" evil antagonists—the corrupt French archaeologist working for the Nazis, the Nazi villain, Belloq (Paul Freeman) who was bent on destroying Indiana and capturing the Lost Ark of the Covenant, and the regiment of Nazi soldiers ordered to deliver the ark to Hitler.

The deal Lucas and Spielberg made with Paramount (the studio that originally turned down *Star Wars*) was virtually unheard of in Hollywood circles. After all the other studios had turned them down, Paramount accepted but only after imposing staggering penalties for going over budget. Consequently, the deal gave Lucas and Spielberg the largest profit margin ever agreed to by a Hollywood film studio.[8]

When the deal was finally set, Spielberg was allied with the young rebel producer-director whom he has admired since his college days. Lucas, however, had to be careful, because Spielberg had not stayed within his budget since *Sugarland Express*. Lucas's concern was magnified by the fact that he had almost gone bankrupt when veteran director Irvin Kershner fell seriously behind schedule with *The Empire Strikes Back* (1980). As producer, Lucas would prove to be conservative with finances and strict about prompt completion of production. As a result, Spielberg could not be as lavish in his methods as he had been with his previous films. He later noted, "beginning with *Raiders* and including *Poltergeist* and *E.T.*, all have been under-schedule and under-budget. I found with these movies that the compromises I made to deliver the films responsibly were actually better than the original ideas I started with. This isn't a rule, and maybe I'll change my mind later, but when I had to make compromises to save some money, I found that the second idea was fresher and better for the movie."[9]

One of the secret weapons Spielberg used to keep ahead of schedule (condescendingly noted by film critic Jonathan Rosenbaum) was his "Hitchcockian storyboard construction"[10] in which the entire film is previsualized and "edited" before production begins. Well educated as a television director, Spielberg did his storyboard homework long before the actual production team assembled to shoot *Raiders*. Spielberg was determined to stay within Lucas's budget and production schedule ("It's hard to spend your friend's money," Spielberg noted),[11] so he decided to storyboard every scene in great detail. Yet, he was not afraid to vary scenes during the shooting if he knew he was ahead of schedule and felt he had the time to deviate from the previsualized storyboard.

Lucas gave Spielberg a shooting schedule of only eighty-five days that included set-ups in four countries. Spielberg later revealed that he actually had two timetables—the original eighty-five-day schedule and his own, which was twelve days shorter.[12] If Indy was going to be the hero of the film, then Spielberg was going to be the hero of the production.

STRUCTURAL ANALYSIS: <u>RAIDERS OF THE LOST ARK</u>

Raiders opens in the jungle with the hero, Indiana Jones (Harrison Ford), making his way toward a hidden temple with a guide. When they reach the cave, Indy kneels down and fills a small cloth pouch with sand and attaches it to his belt. Indy and the guide enter the mouth of the cave cautiously. When Indy breaks a light beam, a poison dart shoots out from the wall and lodges in the wooden staff he is carrying. Next, a spiked gate closes shut; it still bears the corpse of an earlier visitor who came to claim the artifact treasure. The sacred tomb is filled with numerous pitfalls that seem limited only by the scriptwriter's imagination. Spielberg delights in this fantasy and plays it to the hilt.

After entering the sacred chamber where the highly prized Peruvian artifact rests atop a small altar, Indy carefully tests the floor. More hidden traps abound. Loose stones in the floor release poison arrows and darts from the wall. Indy makes his way carefully toward the altar. He finally reaches his goal, studying the artifact to assess its weight, rubbing his chin several times in the process. When the sandbag is readied for the swap, Indy twitches his fingers. Another mimicking sequence follows (reminiscent of Chief Brody's younger son in *Jaws* mimicking his father's drinking with a glass of milk); the guide, entranced in all the suspense, rubs his chin and twitches his fingers in subconscious response to Indy. Indy makes the switch, grabbing the artifact tightly and swapping the sand-filled pouch. He smiles at the thought of his ingenuity, but his smile soon disappears when the stone beneath the pouch suddenly begins to sink into the altar stone. Indy knows that this will trigger a calamity and runs wildly across the deadly floor triggering a barrage of poisonous darts and arrows. Narrowly escaping, he and the guide run toward the mouth of the cave.

During their escape, the floor opens up between the two men. The guide demands the artifact from the trapped Indy, who needs the whip the guide is holding to escape. Indy gives in, throwing the artifact to the guide who, in a traitorous move, drops the whip and escapes through a descending trap door, leaving Indy behind. Indy eventually escapes through the mouth of the cave to safety, but only after being chased by a huge boulder.

Outside the cave, he encouters Belloq (Paul Freeman), now in possession of the artifact, surrounded by the guide and local villagers. When Belloq holds up the artifact to the natives, they bow humbly. Indy sees his chance to escape and runs toward a seaplane where his pilot is waiting.

This ends the first harrowing scene, one that Spielberg purposely constructed to set the film's tone and pace. It relates to nothing in the story that follows, except to establish Indiana's character (even his comic fear of snakes) and introduce his arch rival, Belloq. This scene "ends" a previous unfilmed episode, a technique favored by Lucas who likes to work backward, forward, and sideways, thereby confusing temporal schemes.

The main story actually begins with Indy in his role as an archaeology professor lecturing to his students at an American university. Spielberg introduces Indy's appeal to women with a camera shot of a young female student studying him passionately from her seat. When he turns from the blackboard to address the class, she bats her eyes several times, revealing the message "I Love You," imprinted on her eyelids. Indy does a slight double take, but handles the incident with his usual cool. After the class is over, the museum's curator, Abner, comes to inform Indy that men from the United States Secret Service are waiting to speak with him.

At the meeting, Indy learns of Hitler's plan to resurrect the Lost Ark of the Covenant. He was familiar with the ark through a project he had worked on with a colleague and friend, Professor Ravenwood, years ago. Ravenwood's daughter, Marion (Karen Allen), had fallen in love with Indiana. Indy explains to the secret service men that he and Ravenwood had tried to uncover the ark earlier but, like many others, had been unsuccessful. He shows them a picture of the ark explaining the fire that appears to be coming from it. The search for the ark is of vital importance: *any* army that carries it is invincible! It must be kept from Hitler and the German army.

Indy begins the adventure by boarding a plane for Nepal, hoping to find both Marion and her father. On the plane, a mysterious-looking man peers over his newspaper at Indy. This is Toht (Ronald Lacey), a Nazi stormtrooper assigned to follow Indy and retrieve the much-needed brass medallion crucial to determining the location of the Well of Souls, the resting place for the ark.

In order to give the impression that Indy's flight is long and involved and to make clear his destination, Spielberg and Lucas agreed on the animated map technique—used many times in the old serials—which traces the path of a plane on its route while double-exposing a plane in flight.[13] The map reveals the plane's destination—Nepal—at which point Spielberg cuts to the Ravenwood bar and the film's heroine, Marion.

Marion is seen in a drinking contest with one of the Nepal peasants. Spielberg originally filmed the entire scene in one five-minute take using the highly versatile Louma crane, but this was edited into several cuts to quicken the pace, thereby reducing its running time to approximately two minutes.[14] Marion wins the drinking contest and begins to close the bar. When all the patrons have gone, Indy comes walking through the door like John Wayne entering a saloon. She is surprised to see him, but expressing her anger over their former love affair, she belts him in the mouth. A bloody-lipped Indy learns that Professor Ravenwood, Marion's father, is dead. Indy inquires about the medallion, which once fit atop a staff or pole of a particular length. Marion tells Indy she still has it, but that he will have to come back the next day. He leaves, but only to humor her.

In a 1983 paper delivered to the University Film and Video Association, Barbara L. Baker analyzes Marion's role in *Raiders of the Lost Ark:* "On the surface, the character of Marion seems quite independent. She's feisty, issues commands, swears, shoots guns, hits men, owns her own bar, drinks (and has drinking contests), and basically appears to hold her own. But most of this behavior is in her first scene, and establishes her spunky personality; much of the remaining film undercuts her behavior either verbally or visually."[15]

According to Baker, although Marion is purposely represented as a strong character, she progressively loses her independence as she attempts to win over Indiana. It might be argued that Marion's character is a synthesis of 1940s heroines, but she lacks the charm and finesse of the traditional sensuous heroine of that era. The ambiguities of Marion's character cannot be blamed solely on screenwriter Lawrence Kasdan, since all three—Lucas, Spielberg, and Kasdan—took part in the development of the characters as well as the storyline. Interestingly, Marion's hard-edged independence parallels Princess Leia's (in *Star Wars*). However, where Leia was too serious about her situation, Marion is flippantly cocky—and tomboyish. Ford was more concerned about the resemblance between Indiana Jones and Han Solo. He was afraid that the dialogue written for him in *Empire* would be too close to that in *Raiders*, since Lawrence Kasdan was the scriptwriter for both films; Spielberg concurred and decided to eliminate dialogue that conjured up the other film.[17]

When the head Nazi stormtrooper, Toht, enters the bar after Indy has left, Marion becomes less "uppity," less confident, and more concerned. Toht has also come for the medallion and demands it immediately. When she tells Toht and his henchmen to leave, Toht threatens her with a hot poker. She is rescued by Indiana, who comes crashing onto the scene with his whip, snatching the hot poker from Toht's hands. When the poker lands on nearby curtains the Ravenwood bar is set ablaze. Meanwhile, Indiana fights off Toht and his comrades. (This is the first time Spielberg uses pyrotechnics extensively.)

During the fight, Marion pauses to drink from a punctured barrel before clobbering one of Toht's thugs. These small touches are characteristic of Spielberg's wit and charm. Although criticized for his lack of characterization, Spielberg still manages to keep his characters enjoyable. In all his films he likes to offset intense action by giving a light comic touch to his characters. Like George Lucas, he always thinks of his audience first.

Toward the end of the fight, Toht discovers the brass medallion in some burning wood. He attempts to retrieve the medallion but burns his hand in the process. (The medallion leaves its impression in Toht's skin, so that it can be reconstructed later by the Nazis.) Toht, however, escapes the skirmish and disappears. While Marion's bar is burning to the ground, she turns to Indiana and says, "we're partners now." With nothing to keep her there, she leaves Nepal with Indy.

Indiana and Marion travel together to Cairo, where they meet up with Sallah (John Rhys-Davies), a friend of Indy's and "the best digger in Cairo." Indy discusses the possibilities of finding the ark with Sallah. Sallah informs Indy that the Germans have been digging for it near Tannis and have found the map room. Indy shows the brass medallion to Sallah, who warns "maybe man was not meant to disturb it. . . . death always surrounds the ark!"

When Indiana and Marion tour Cairo, they are followed by the Nazis and natives working for them. Eventually, Indiana and Marion are attacked by these natives wielding swords. Indy puts Marion in a haywagon to hide her while he continues the fight. As the haywagon moves through the streets, Marion jumps off and finds herself being chased. She hides in a tall wicker basket. The small pet monkey first seen at Sallah's home jumps on the basket, giving her hiding place away. Just when Indy thinks he has fought them all off, a large, ominous Arab in black appears wielding a large swashbuckler sword. Indy, frustrated, pulls out his gun and kills him (Spielberg later commented that Harrison Ford was suffering from a bad case of diarrhea and this was the quickest way to wrap up the scene without prolonging Ford's uncomfortable time on the set.)[18] Indy hears Marion crying out from a basket, but he doesn't know which one. He pushes over numerous wicker baskets but never finds Marion. Finally, he sees the Nazis putting a similar wicker basket on an explosives truck. When the truck explodes, Indy believes Marion is dead.

A meeting in a Cairo bar with Belloq ensues. He explains to Indy (a disbeliever) that the ark is a "radio transmitter" allowing men to talk with God. He wants to engage Indy's help, offering to split the prize for finding the ark, but Indy refuses. Pining at the thought of Marion's tragic fate, he continues to play with the monkey and slowly gets drunk.

Sallah reports that the Nazis have a copy of the brass medallion and Indy is perplexed at how they obtained such a replica, since presumably there were no copies (it was from Toht's burned hand). The writing on one side of the medallion gives a warning from God, while the other side (the side Toht's burned hand did not possess) contains the measurements of and placement for the staff in the map room. Indy realizes that Belloq's staff is too long and surmises they still do not know the correct location of the Well of Souls.

Sallah and Indy then go to the site of Tannis, where the ark is supposedly hidden. Dressed as Arabs, Indy and Sallah make their way undetected to the map room. Sallah lowers Indy into the room where Indy deciphers the inscription on the stone floor to locate the position of the staff. As the angle of the sun shifts, the beam of light, now magnified by the stone in the medallion, is directed onto the floor where a miniature replica of the lost city lies. The beam of light reveals the location of the Well of Souls as a burst of searing sunlight floods the scene. Sallah and Indy then seek out the Well of Souls. Along the way, to avoid several Nazis they duck into a tent and unsuspectingly find Marion. She is not dead after all, but in true serial tradition, is bound, gagged, and tied to a tent pole. She immediately wants him to free her. Though glad to see her, Indy realizes that if the Nazis find her gone, his presence at Tannis will be detected and his plan to seize the ark foiled. Instead of untying her, he gags her again and leaves. Marion, of course, is furious!

Sallah, Indy, and some of Sallah's friends make their way to the Well of Souls. After digging a while, they find the opening into the chamber containing the ark. A torch is dropped into the chamber and Sallah asks why the floor is moving. On closer inspection, Indiana realizes what is moving and replies, "why does it have to be snakes?" Indiana and Sallah are lowered into the chamber filled with snakes. A cobra rears its head at Indy, who is terrified at the sight (his one and only phobia—set up in the opening sequence).

Marion, meanwhile, is being entertained by Belloq. He unveils a new white dress for her (we wonder, of course, where he obtained such a dress for this supposedly spontaneous visit—or did he plan it all along?). It is his attempt to get information from her that might help him locate the secret chamber containing the ark. She attempts to lure him into a drinking contest. Belloq becomes drunk, but so does Marion. She pulls a knife on him, but both laugh drunkenly. Marion's attempt to run away is foiled when Toht sneaks into the tent and stops her.

By this time, Sallah and Indiana have raised the ark out of the chamber. Belloq, suspecting that Indy is near the digging site, commands the German officer Dietrich (Wolf Kahler) and a group of soldiers to find him. Belloq and Dietrich eventually do. When Indy looks up, he sees Belloq staring down at him. Belloq orders Marion into the chamber with Indiana. She falls on the dirt floor only to be greeted by the cobra, which had reared up at Indy earlier. Indy and Marion appear doomed!

All looks hopeless, but Indiana figures that the secret chamber is probably connected to other chambers already excavated by the Nazis. He climbs on a tall statue, rocking it from its foundations. It crashes into another wall through which

Indiana and Marion try to escape. Then, noticing the plane (Flying Wing) that the Nazis have brought in to fly out the ark, Indy springs into action. (The Flying Wing cost the production company approximately sixty thousand dollars; it was constructed at EMI Elstree studios, disassembled, and flown to the Tunisia location for filming.)[19]

Indy reaches the plane and fights off a Nazi guard. The ruckus draws the attention of a large Nazi soldier who is looking for a good fight. Marion also makes her way to the plane, where she subdues the pilot (the producer of *Raiders*, Frank Marshall, in a bit part) and takes over the plane's machine gun. During the scrap, Indy cleverly lures the Nazi into the plane's propeller, which promptly chops him to pieces. Flames from the gas truck punctuated by Marion's gun fire are licking toward the plane. Indy wisks Marion off the plane before it blows up.

Sallah finds Indy and Marion and tells them that the Nazis have loaded the ark on a truck destined for Cairo. As the truck and its escort pull away, Indy jumps on a white horse—John Wayne style—and begins pursuit. In another unusual move in his career—necessitated by the shooting schedule—Spielberg allowed Mickey Moore to direct a second unit crew made up of professional stunt men headed by stunt coordinator Glenn Randall, Jr. It took the crew two weeks to film the chase sequence. Moore followed Spielberg's storyboards carefully, since the close-up action with Harrison Ford later filmed by Spielberg himself and the shots had to match. It works very well, and is one of the film's most famous sequences.

In a breathtaking chase scene, Indy jumps from a cliff onto the truck and climbs into its cab, killing the Nazi driver. He runs several escort vehicles off the road at various stages of the chase. The men guarding the ark in the back of the truck try to make their way to the cab, but Indy shakes them off by swerving the truck to and fro. Eventually, one Nazi makes it into the cab and throws Indy through the windshield. He narrowly escapes death by grabbing a hood ornament, but it bends and falls under the truck. To escape certain death, he allows himself to be dragged by the truck underneath. He makes his way to the truck's rear axle, where he attaches his whip and is dragged from behind. He finally pulls himself back onto the rear of the truck by the whip, works his way to the cab, and returns the favor—he throws the Nazi through the broken windshield. The Nazi is crushed in the process. Indy drives the truck with the ark into Cairo, where Sallah and his men are waiting to hide it.

Sallah has arranged passage on a ship and Indy and Marion set sail. In the film's only "love" scene, Marion attempts to salve Indy's injuries but he falls asleep. It is typical of Spielberg to play such a scene for laughs, and it fits in with Lucas's own style, since neither filmmaker uses sex much in his films. Spielberg has commented that he may someday do an "adult" movie, but he would have the lovers "laugh themselves to orgasm."[20]

When the ship stops dead in the ocean, Indy realizes that something is wrong. A Nazi sub has stopped the ship and stormtroopers have boarded. He hides while Marion is taken by the Nazis and put aboard the submarine. When the Nazi sub departs, Indiana swims to the sub and boards it, knocking a Nazi unconscious and stealing his uniform.

When the sub reaches its destination, a small island in the middle of nowhere, Belloq convinces Dietrich to open the ark before it is delivered to Hitler. The Nazi soldiers are delivering the ark to a secluded part of the island when Indy appears on a cliff with a bazooka aimed at the ark. He tells Dietrich to let Marion go, but Belloq appeals to the archaeologist in Indy. Just as curious about the ark's contents as Belloq, he puts down the bazooka. The Nazis march to a small grotto where the ark is placed, ready for opening. Indy and Marion are tied to a stake at the opposite end of the grotto when Belloq and Dietrich give the command to open the ark. The lid is lifted and Belloq reaches in only to discover a handful of sand. The stone tablets have disintegrated!

For the next ten minutes, Spielberg unleashes the power of the ark through a variety of unique and original special effects created by Lucas's Industrial Light and Magic staff in California. When Belloq gazes into the ark, he is besieged with ghostly images and begins to scream in horror. A wand of smoke emanates from the ark and drifts toward the Nazis standing at attention. A piercing bolt of lightning strikes each Nazi through the heart one after the other. Toht's head, along with the heads of several other Nazis, appears to melt, then explode.

When the fireworks from the ark begin, Indiana tells Marion not to look. This appears to contradict Indy's belief that it is all "hokus-pokus," but it is reminiscent of the biblical tale where Lot tells his wife not to watch the destruction of Sodom.

When the Nazis are dead, a blast of fire shoots out from the ark and into the sky toward heaven. The process then reverses itself; the fire is swallowed up by the ark and the lid shuts tight again.

For the final scene, Spielberg cuts to a lonely warehouse worker in the act of storing the ark in a box marked "top secret." Spielberg pulls back his camera to reveal a huge warehouse filled with thousands of similar boxes, an obvious tribute to Orson Welles's *Citizen Kane*. This scene was just one of several that employed "motion control," a sophisticated computerized system that synchronizes a moving foreground scene with a matted, moving background. (Prior to this system, the camera could not move when it filmed the foreground action.) All camera movements executed while filming the foreground action are stored in a computer's memory (and eventually in a mass storage medium such as a computer tape or diskette). The computer is then used to control the process camera filming the background plate to be matted. Since these movements are synchronized with the original photography, both foreground and background shots (which make up the composite scene) "move" in unison and appear very realistic. For Steven Spielberg, *Raiders of the Lost Ark* became his "ride at Disneyland, inexpensive but believable."[21]

ANOTHER BOX-OFFICE FIRST

Lucas was at one time interested in futuristic (but realistic) science fiction (*THX 1138*), but he sidestepped into futuristic space fantasy with the *Star Wars* series. By comparison, Spielberg appeared to be working toward a synthesis of diverse film modes. His work seemed to combine the innocence, wonder, and magic of Walt Disney with traditional American stories told by film's greatest directors—John Ford, Alfred Hitchcock, and Frank Capra. Spielberg's films recalled the traditional Hollywood drama of a bygone era: action and adventure moderated by the warm touch of Disney and the animated frenzy of Chuck Jones and Hanna-Barbera. The product of the Lucas-Spielberg collaboration (which Tony Crawley dubbed "Lucasberger") is a fascinating hybrid that proved to be a major financial success. The structure, episodic in nature like that of the *Star Wars* trilogy, guarantees future installments of Indiana Jones of which four were originally planned.[22] The huge success of *Raiders of the Lost Ark* prepared the way for Lucas's next Indiana Jones adventure, *Indiana Jones and the Temple of Doom*, a story based on the ideas of Lucas and a screenplay by writer Willard Huyck and Gloria Katz, who scripted *American Graffiti*.

Spielberg was offered the sequel to *Jaws*, but his instincts proved correct in turning the project down. He had given his best on the original and was aware that a sequel is usually never as good nor as well received by audiences. The Indiana Jones situation was, however, different. Spielberg had enjoyed his experience working with Lucas and reported: "I had separation pangs. I knew if I didn't direct [*Temple of Doom*], somebody else would. I got a little bit jealous, I got a little bit frustrated, and I signed on for one more."[23] In an interview with Suzanne Harper after the release of *Temple of Doom*, Spielberg explained the problems of making a sequel: "the danger in making a sequel is that you can never satisfy everyone. If you give people the same movie with different scenes, they say, "Why weren't you more original? But if you give them the same character in another fantastic adventure, but with a different *tone*, you risk disappointing the other half of the audience, who just wanted a carbon copy of the first film with a different girl and a different bad guy. So you win and you lose both ways."[24]

Spielberg began planning *Temple of Doom* in January 1983 and was set to begin production in May of that year. The new cast included a former schoolteacher, Kate Capshaw, who played the heroine. The pace of this movie is much more vigorous than *Raiders*—apparently because Spielberg was afraid of boring his audience. Indeed, he never gave movie patrons a chance to breathe; *Newsweek* reviewer Jack Kroll claims: "Spielberg has gone to such lengths to avoid boredom that he has leaped squarely into the opposite trap: this movie has such unrelenting action that it jackhammers you into a punch-drunk stupor."[25] Interestingly, Spielberg predicted, "its going to have the same velocity as the first movie, and the humor and tempo are the same."[26] He obviously delivered more than he originally promised.

STRUCTURAL ANALYSIS: TEMPLE OF DOOM

For the next installment of Indiana Jones, George Lucas turned the clock back one year to 1935. The film opens with the logo of Paramount Pictures (a mountain flanked by clouds) embossed on a large brass oriental gong, a tribute to George Stevens's epic film *Gunga Din* (1939). But there the parallel stops for, according to Kroll's *Newsweek* review, "Stevens's movie . . . lifted you out of your seat with exhilaration. The temple scenes in [Spielberg's] 'Indiana Jones' grind you into your seat with a kind of animal embarrassment."[27] Indy is teamed up with nightclub singer Willie Scott (Kate Capshaw) and Short Round (Ke Huy Quan), a streetwise kid who is Indy's sidekick in this adventure. The film begins with Willie singing a broken English-Chinese version of Cole Porter's "Anything Goes" in a Shanghai nightclub. Kroll sums up

Spielberg's opening scene this way: "After the clever opening number, Willie is thrown together with that adventurous archaeologist, Indiana Jones (Harrison Ford), facing off with a tableful of Chinese hoods who are trying to eliminate him with revolvers (no way), machine guns (try again) and poison (possible). The result is an epic melee that seems choreographed by some crazy mutation of Mack Sennett and Twyla Tharp."[28]

In the midst of this commotion the plot begins. Indy has found the jade urn containing the ashes of Lao Che's royal ancestor Nurchachi. He wants to trade it for a large diamond that Lao possesses. Lao, however, double-crosses Indy by poisoning his cocktail. He offers Indy a lifesaving antidote in exchange for the urn. When Indy's head begins to swell and his vision blur, he makes a futile attempt to secure the antidote. A fight results, and both the diamond and the vial of antidote are knocked to the floor where they are kicked and shuffled endlessly between Willie (chasing the diamond) and Indy (chasing the vial). At one point, Willie nearly grabs the gem, but loses it when a large bucket of ice cubes is knocked over. Both Indy and Willie escape behind the giant rolling gong, but not before Indy secures the much-needed vial. They both jump out a window to a waiting car below. Behind the wheel is Short Round, Indy's companion, ready to whisk them through the narrow streets of Shanghai. When the car turns the corner, we see the marquee of the club Indy and Willie were in, "Club Obi Wan," a sly tribute to Lucas's *Star Wars*.

At the airport, the unsuspecting threesome, thinking they have escaped the villains, climb aboard a plane headed toward Siam. When the door shuts, the logo of the plane is revealed—it is of Lao's airfreight company and the pilots are Lao's paid hoods. During the flight, Willie begins to make a fuss about her current inconvenience, but Indy (in true form) ignores her and goes to sleep. Later, when Indy, Willie, and Short Round are asleep, Lao's pilots dump the fuel from the gas tanks and quietly walk toward the back of the plane, where they parachute to safety. Indy wakes up when the engines sputter and the plane falls into a tailspin. When they realize that none of them can fly a plane, Indy springs into action. Stretching credulity a bit, Spielberg has the threesome exit the plane in an inflatable rubber raft. They land successfully on a mountainside and toboggan down a steep slope, landing in wild river rapids. The raft finally comes to a gentle stop at the base of the Mayapore hills in India and the pilotless plane crashes into a side of a mountain. Although many of Indiana's adventures are believable (mandated by Lucas), in this film the character does lapse occasionally into superhuman feats thanks to director Spielberg. After all, Indy is a serial type character. But Lucas felt that since Indy possesses human weaknesses and lacks superhuman powers, his adventures should be kept within realistic boundaries. During preproduction on *Raiders*, Spielberg commented, "He [Lucas] would say, 'That's going to be hard to swallow.' And he was right."[29] Huyck and Katz's adventure comic-book script set up situations for its hero that were not as realistic as Kasdan's in *Raiders*.

Indy, Willie, and Short Round are met by an elderly shaman who leads them to his nearby village, an ominous, uninviting place. The shaman informs Indy that the village has been under a curse since the Maharajah of Pankot had its sacred stone confiscated. The shaman explains—to Indy's disbelief—that the missing stone has caused the crops to wither and animals to die. In addition, the children have mysteriously disappeared.

Indiana is sympathetic, but he is anxious to travel to Delhi, where he can catch a plane to America. Just as they prepare to leave for Delhi, one of the village children appears, having escaped from Pankot. This changes Indy's mind and, despite Willie's frantic protests, the three travel to Pankot Palace to meet with the maharajah, a thirteen-year-old boy.

Indy, Willie, and Short Round are escorted to Pankot Palace via elephant and local guides. During the journey, Willie is constantly complaining: to smother the acute odor of the elephant, Willie sprinkles the beast with perfume; during a rest stop while Willie is trying to change Indy's mind about the expedition, her elephant takes a fancy for her and begins affectionately caressing her with its trunk. Capshaw's words recount the experience: "It wasn't hard to play Willie Scott, who is always bitching about things, because it *was* hot, the bugs *were* disgusting and the elephant was a pain in the butt."[30] When they finally reach the palace, they are invited to a feast that includes a variety of unusual foods. This oddly adolescent episode (noted by reviewers as typical of both Lucas and Spielberg, but extreme even for them) is described in *Newsweek* as "a grossout banquet scene in the palace of a sinister child rajah, featuring such delicacies as snake, live eels, fried beetles, eyeball chowder and chilled monkey brains." It is here that, as the reviewer comments, "the throttle is being turned up and when we reach the temple of doom there's a turbocharged zoom into overkill."[31] After the feast, Indy, Willie, and Short Round retire for the evening. The romance between Willie and Indiana begins to heat up, but as in *Raiders*, Spielberg resists the temptation and opts instead for a diversion. Their "affair" is interrupted, unexpectedly, by an assassin. Indy immediately dispenses the intruder and then searches for his place of entry. He uncovers a false wall that opens into a secret passage. Short Round, awake from all the commotion, follows Indy into the passageway while Willie stays behind.

The passage is inhabited by an assortment of disgusting insects (again seemingly added merely for gross effect). As Indy and Short Round move into another chamber, Indy accidentally activates a booby trap. Long, sharp spikes appear from both ceiling and floor, and the ceiling begins to lower on them. They yell for help. Hearing their desperate cries, Willie enters the passageway amid all the hideous crawlers. In a wonderfully crafted scene, Spielberg exhibits the same tension and excitement that were present in *Raiders* when Indy found himself trying to escape the booby traps in the Peruvian cave. Willie, meanwhile, makes it to the outside of the chamber and trips the mechanism; Indy and Short Round have barely escaped death.

Spielberg employs an overlap action editing technique here and in other death-defying episodes in the film. The same technique had been used in *Raiders*. It is a style of editing that was used to enhance the suspense and drama in films made during the thirties, forties, and early fifties. Students engaged in film studies are often shown the early fifties episodes of "Gunsmoke," where this technique was used for shoot-outs, stagecoach chases, and other action scenes. It produces a barely noticeable overlap of the action. It not only causes the audience to focus on a particular action but also prolongs the action for dramatic effect. The technique is no longer used in contemporary filmmaking where scenes are cut on matched action.

The trio finally makes its way through a twisting tunnel into the subterranean Temple of Doom. Observing from a safe distance, they witness a Thuggee ceremony conducted by the high priest Mola Ram. In a lurid sequence beyond the wildest dreams of Saturday afternoon serial fans, Ram and the worshipers perform a human sacrifice dedicated to the bloodthirsty goddess Kali. Overlooking a pit looms a large statue of Kali that holds the three sacred altar stones. During the sacrifice, Ram plunges his hand into his victim and pulls out his heart. Apparently still alive (somehow) the sacrificial victim is lowered into a molten pit created by Lucas's Industrial Light and Magic staff. When the lava burns the victim alive, the camera cuts to Ram holding the victim's heart, which bursts into flames.

When the worshipers vacate the temple, Indy descends into the temple to retrieve the magic stones. Indy is aware that there are five stones altogether, two of which have been lost in the subterranean caves. When Indiana grabs the stones and places them in a satchel, he is caught by Thuggee guards who work in the underground mines. Short Round is also caught and thrown into the cell with Indy.

Indiana is then brought before the high priest, Ram, who unveils his evil plans. He tells Indy that the children are in the mines digging for the two remaining sacred stones. Once they are found, the stones' awesome power will be released and Mola Ram and his followers will expand their evil influence until Kali, their goddess, rules the world. After hearing Ram's plan, Indy is forced to drink the blood of Kali, which puts him under an evil spell.

Willie, who has also been caught, is brought to the pit. Indy, under Ram's evil spell, helps to ready Willie for the sacrifice. Meanwhile, Short Round, who has been forced to work in the mines with the children, learns from them that pain caused by fire can "wake up" a person from the wicked spell. In a daring escape from the mines, Short Round reaches the sacrificial pit where Willie is being lowered and, in a desperate attempt to wake Indy out of the spell, shoves a burning torch in his side. Indy regains his senses and saves Willie from the pit.

Again in possession of the Sankara stones, Indy helps free the children from the mines. They begin their own escape to the surface. Along the way, they free from his trance the boy maharajah, who then runs off to secure help from the British forces. Indy, Willie, and Short Round make their own daring escape in a mining car. It's *Rollercoaster* on a small scale, but effectively choreographed by Spielberg, who uses just about every gimmick and gag Mack Sennett used in his railroad chase sequences. Film buffs and reviewers have compared this sequence to scenes from *The General.*

Spielberg, no stranger to coordinating miniature shots (recall *1941*), believes that "sometimes it's better to do things in miniature as opposed to full size."[32] So, in addition to a full-scale mine car railway system constructed at Elstree Studios, a miniature railway set was used. It was built by Dennis Muren, visual special effects supervisor. Muren said, "In shooting the miniatures [in stop motion animation], we used Nikon still cameras . . . with 30 feet of Vistavision film shooting at one frame per second. . . . We shot single frame stop motion so that Tom St. Amand could animate the puppets [about 10 inches tall] each shot, and eventually Bruce Nicholson, who did the optical work, put a little "shake" into each element. This matched in with the live action footage shot in England on the full sized set."[33]

While the mine car chase is in progress, followers of Ram topple the supports of a large underground cistern, which releases a monstrous tidal wave into the mine passageways. Indy, Willie, and Short Round make a break for it when they hear the thunderous sounds of water. They leave the tunnel just as the rushing water spews from the mineshaft into the crocodile-infested river gorge below. Standing on a small ledge, they can escape only by means of a rope bridge heavily guarded by Ram's Thuggees. In a scene reminiscent of dozens of Hollywood B movies, Indy fights them off and cuts the rope bridge. Most of the villains fall, and Indy, still fighting one or two, climbs to safety. The enslaved children are seen running free from the temple. Indy, Willie, and Short Round return to the Mayapore, where they replace the sacred stone on the small altar, and Indiana Jones is off to still another adventure yet to be filmed!

CRITICISM

The major criticism of *Temple of Doom* focuses on what appeared to most reviewers to be its excessive violence and horror. The complaint is unusual in an era noted for graphic depiction of violence in films, such as *Taxi Driver* (1976) and *Scarface* (1984). Although screen violence is now commonplace, it was a shock coming from Spielberg and Lucas, whose audiences are mainly young. One reviewer calls it "an astonishing violation of the trust people have in Spielberg and Lucas's essentially good-natured approach to movies intended primarily for kids."[34] George Will, in his syndicated newspaper column, said of the film "suddenly it becomes ugly."[35] Kroll found the rhythms of the film got "out of hand"

and suggested the underground railway chase was akin to "kinetic pornography—quantity annihilating quality."[36]

Temple of Doom changed Spielberg's saccharine image (created by *Close Encounters* and *E.T.*) as a filmmaker for children. His other 1984 film project, *Gremlins* (for which he served as producer for director Joe Dante) also created justifiable distrust in the minds of parents and reviewers who had seen Spielberg as the Walt Disney of the eighties. *Gremlins*, although advertised with cute pictures that appealed to small children, lacks the good-natured tone of Spielberg's earlier films. It reinforced the pressure to create a new rating for children under thirteen (as noted earlier this was passed in 1984 with Spielberg's full support).

Spielberg was aware of the violence in *Temple of Doom* but dodged critics' charges by claiming he was "only a 'hired hand.'"[37] He justifies Katz and Huyck's script by saying: "George . . . felt that he wanted this second Indiana Jones movie to contain moments of black magic, truly evil villains. Certainly you could say that the villains in the last film were evil, but they dealt in simple force. In this movie, our villains deal in black magic, torture, and slavery. So they're *real* bad."[38]

The question most critics raised after seeing the latest installment of Indiana Jones, is what could the archaeologist do next? He appears to have done it all, prompting George Will to state, "whatever else art involves, it involves proportionality and subtlety—the ability to approach the edge of success without falling in . . . and that is why there may not be a third Indy epic."[39]

7 / "I'm Going to Make You a Star"

Dear E.T.,

I love you and want you to come to my house on Christmas Day and spend the night with me in case I get scared. E.T. I love you.

Love,
Heidi
Letters to E.T., 1983

Spielberg, with the help of special effects wizard Carlo Rambaldi and hundreds of artists and technicians, decided literally to make a star for his next film, *E.T.: The Extra-Terrestrial.* Described by Paul Sammon as "a squat, wrinkled, mud-colored beastie with a perpetual chest cold," E.T. was the unlikely popular and media sensation of 1982.[1] This ugly, but endearing electronic-mechanical alien graced everything from the cover of *Rolling Stone* (he was bumped from the covers of other major national magazines only by the Falklands War) to bedsheets (carefully licensed, of course, for marketing by Spielberg's business and legal branches). The most remarkable thing about this "star" is that he is an illusion. With this film, Spielberg brings to culmination his spellbinding technique, hiding it "so well that never once are you taken out of your chair and reminded of where you are."[2]

More lifelike than his ancestor King Kong (also crafted by Rambaldi for the 1976 remake), E.T., according to Sammon, was a combination of special effects, mechanics, electronics, and actors, including a mime and two midgets. Rambaldi, who "made a number of E.T.s for the film," claims,

Mainly, however, we depended on three different ones throughout the filming. One was a lightweight electro-mechanical form which we bolted to the stage floor and which was capable of thirty points of movement in the face and thirty more in the body. Another, more complicated, body was auto-electronic. When they needed a close-up or something sophisticated, they usually brought out the electronic E.T., which had eighty-six separate points of movement—the most I ever put into a figure. Even King Kong only had forty. And this electronic E.T. had a lot of servo boxes hanging off it and many more cables than the mechanical E.T.

The third suit, cableless and capable of only ten points of movement was custom-designed and padded to be worn by little people for E.T.'s walking scenes. The other, non-walking shots—eighty-five percent of E.T.'s total screen time—exclusively featured the electronic and mechanical models. The primary "little people" suit was also fitted with radio-controlled arms.[3]

Rambaldi also created four complicated E.T. heads and working parts. Many of the other special effects for the film were created by George Lucas's subsidiary company, Industrial Light and Magic.

Spielberg said he wanted "a creature that only a mother could love. I didn't want him to be sublime or beatific—or there'd be no place to go in the relationship. The story is the beauty of [E.T.'s] character."[4] Rambaldi's final result, however, exceeded Spielberg's expectations and caused him to exclaim, "E.T. could have sung arias if he'd wanted to."[5]

Most critics agree that E.T.'s performance—considering the limitations of any electro-mechanical creation—was beautifully choreographed. Spielberg took a chance that the inherent personality of the alien, created by the script, would help to overshadow any visual imperfections that might show through. Everything depended on the alien's believability and characterization. Critics were not enthusiastic about Spielberg's mechanical creature in *Jaws*, noting that the close-ups of the latex shark at the end of the film almost destroyed the illusion Spielberg was trying to create (even Spielberg's uncertainty caused him to conceal the shark for most of the film); Rambaldi's Puck in *Close Encounters*—Spielberg's vision of what earthlings might see during their first meeting with extraterrestrials—fared much better, but it was only on the screen for a short time at the end of the film.[6] But E.T. became a star, and Spielberg was nominated for an Academy Award for his directorial efforts (his other nominations were for *Close Encounters* and *Raiders*).

BACKGROUND

Many Spielberg fans, as well as critics, expected something like *E.T.: The Extra-Terrestrial* to come along sooner than the summer of 1982. During a press conference after the premiere of *Close Encounters of the Third Kind* in the fall of 1977, Spielberg indicated that he had plans for a sequel, but he was vague in his discussion of the outline of the story.[7] As Tony Crawley notes, "The director [of *Close Encounters*] had always said he hoped Richard Dreyfuss's Common Man would be returned to earth by Puck and the other aliens."[8] That idea never materialized, especially after Spielberg decided to re-edit and reshoot additional material for the special edition. What began as an idea for the sequel to *Close Encounters* developed into the initial idea for *E.T.: The Extra-Terrestrial*, but slowly and with several changes in both director and screenwriters. It is not surprising, therefore, that *E.T.* exhibits the friendly alien scenario, the heavy use of Disney-like fantasy, and Spielberg's own personal vision of extra-terrestrial life already seen in *Close Encounters*.

By 1979, Spielberg had written a story entitled "Night Skies," which he turned over to screenwriter John Sayles for further development. Ron Cobb, an art director who helped on several scenes in both John Carpenter's *Dark Star* (1974) and George Lucas's *Star Wars* (1977), was set to direct; the

new aliens were to be designed by Rick Baker, a talented
makeup artist who worked on the remake of *King Kong* (1976)
and later on John Landis's *American Werewolf in London*
(1981).[9] At this point, Spielberg appeared comfortable in acting as producer for a work that he initially created. However,
difficulties arose and the "Night Skies" idea was in trouble:
"'The basic idea came from Spielberg's research on *Close Encounters,*' reported John Sayles, 'involving a kind of an isolated farmhouse. I thought of it as *Drums Along the Mohawk*
(1939), with extra-terrestrials instead of Indians.' Rick Baker
saw it more like *Straw Dogs* (1971), which could explain many
of the changes to come. Spielberg is no Sam Peckinpah."[10]

The initial problem with the film was its large budget. For
this reason, Sayles cut his eleven alien creatures to five in the
screenplay, but Columbia found the project still too expensive. As Sayles recalls: "I did one draft . . . [and] we talked
about it, and I started a revision while Rick Baker began de-
signs for the extra-terrestrials . . . five as I remember. The second draft came in, people seemed pretty pleased and I lost
track of the project while it went through Columbia for bud-
geting. The next I heard, Columbia had passed on it, osten-
sibly because of what it would cost; and Spielberg and
Rick Baker had fallen out, also because of financial
disagreements."[11]

Spielberg also had reservations about Sayles's script,
which portrayed the aliens, especially the alien leader, Scar,
as hostile to humans. Crawley notes that Spielberg was more
interested in the smallest (and friendliest) alien in Sayles's
group, which led him to the idea "What if he got left behind?
What if the little chap, the straggler, missed the bus home."[12]
When the "Night Skies" project fell apart, Spielberg returned
to *Close Encounters* in the hope that Columbia would be satisfied with a special edition of the film in lieu of a sequel.

Spielberg supposedly conceived *E.T.: The Extra-Terrestrial*
while filming *Raiders.* Crawley notes that he had been working on two horror films for the summer trade:

What he was planning, by way of antithesis, was a couple of shock-horror numbers, *Poltergeist* and *Night Skies*. A pair of quicky productions, good for summer trade. What he did do was read the second script more often than the first, notice how it related in many ways to the first. Then he discovered within it the kernel of antithesis to both shockers. . . . Why not merge the second with some previous thoughts and bring in some kids . . . and it, or *E.T.*, built on from there. . . . The antecedents of *E.T.* are about the most convoluted of any Spielberg film. It grew out of three scripts, four writers, six titles and two special effects wizards, every bit as much as out of the Spielbergian soul.[13]

One of Spielberg's more useful talents is his ability to connect the right idea with the right people. With *E.T.*, Spielberg connected a dissatisfied writer with an idea that developed into her most famous screenplay to date. Because of his interest in Puck, Spielberg discussed story possibilities with screenwriter Melissa Mathison, who had come to visit Harrison Ford on the set of *Raiders* (she later married him). Earlier, Kathleen Kennedy (the coproducer of *E.T.*) had suggested Mathison, who had written the screenplay for *The Black Stallion* (1979). Initially Mathison refused, because, according to Crawley, she had reread her recent work and decided never to write again.[14] Later, while the filming of *Raiders* continued in Tunisia, Spielberg told Mathison that he wanted to make a film about children who discover an alien from outer space.[15] This time she was interested and agreed to write the script. She was a perfect choice since her writing added a female perspective to Spielberg's story. It is interesting to note that most of the production staff were also women.[16] This may explain why *E.T.* lacks the hard edge of Spielberg's previous work, where critics accused him of making "brilliant movies with a mechanical heart."[17]

Spielberg's technical virtuosity separates him from other directors in his class. His direction of special effects wizards and cameramen creates a cinematic visual whole that elevates an improbable premise to a believable product. His choice of cameraman for *E.T.* was Allen Daviau, whom he had used on his first 35-mm short, *Amblin'*. Daviau created a series of lighting motifs that accented the various scenes appropriately. In keeping with Spielberg's lighting trademark, that of slight diffusion coupled with heavy backlighting and the use of weak fill lights, Charles Michener and Katrine Ames observe: "'E.T.' achieves its almost hypnotic hold through the much more subtly manipulative play of light, which Spielberg and his cinematographer, Allen Daviau, orchestrate like symphonic motifs: the lush darkness of the forest contrasts with the flat brightness of the suburban community; a kind of holy back light bathes Elliott and the E.T. whereas Elliott's family—his mother, little sister and older brother—are viewed in natural, all-around light; the black silhouettes of the advancing government forces suddenly blaze into clinical fluorescence after they find E.T. in his hideaway."[18]

While in development at Columbia Pictures, *E.T.* was thought of as a "kiddie" picture. The Columbia executives' favorite project at the time—one that they felt had more of a story and, more importantly, blockbuster appeal—was John Carpenter's *Starman*, finally filmed in 1984. By several twists of fate, Spielberg's film project was dropped by Columbia and picked up by Universal, whereas Carpenter's film was put on hold at Columbia for several years.

ANALYSIS

For his most successful film to date, Spielberg decided to "wing *E.T.*," that is, to improvise.[19] This was an unusual move for Spielberg, whose meticulous storyboarding usually precedes production. The effect of this preproduction work, as some critics have noted, created interesting, yet mechanical films that provided the fast pace sought by a television generation audience. But the procedure entails a lack of spontaneity; and the resulting product usually appears suspiciously crafted; many of Spielberg's works are carefully contrived, devoid of "holes" or lulls in the action. With *E.T.*, Spielberg decided on a new approach: "Winging *E.T.* made it a very spontaneous, vital movie. . . . I realized I didn't need the drawings for a small movie like *E.T.* I would never wing *Raiders II*, but I could improvise a more personal picture like *E.T.*, which was essentially more about people and relationships."[20]

The *E.T.* story is simple and straightforward, an interesting cross between *The Greatest Story Ever Told* (1965) and *Old Yeller* (1957), with a bit of *Peter Pan*. *Time* reviewer Richard Corliss describes it as "a miracle movie, and one that confirms Spielberg as a master storyteller of his medium."[21] The film starts where John Sayles's "Night Skies"screenplay ends—the friendly alien is left behind after his spaceship takes off from earth. The ancient alien's adoption by three typically suburban children, his adventures on earth, and his subsequent return home provide the plot. For one of the children in particular, Elliott (Henry Thomas), E.T. represents a special friend, providing him companionship that has been all but lost because his father has left the family and his mother works. He is also separated from his brother, Michael, who has his own older friends, and from his little sister, Gertie, by her youth and feminine interests. It is a story of a "shy, lonely boy in desperate need of a friend—when suddenly one falls out of the sky."[22]

It is Elliott who discovers the "goblin" in the backyard shed and lures him into the house with Reese's Pieces. Once in his room, E.T. begins scanning the various toys and objects scattered around. It becomes a learning process between an old alien and an earthbound boy. Spielberg develops a touching tale that all kids—especially suburban children as Spielberg was—might fantasize during those lonely, isolated periods of youth.

From this point, Spielberg builds a variety of experiences for E.T. and Elliott to share. As Michener and Ames note, "It is through this friendship that Elliott finds a way out of his closed-up anger and discovers the promise of real manhood in a series of funny, touching, exhilarating and, finally, shattering scenes."[23] E.T.'s glowing finger, we learn, can heal Elliott's cut finger. E.T.'s heartlight causes his chest to glow at various times, either in dire fear or because he has been warmly touched. There is also a symbiotic relationship between the creature and the boy, so that whatever E.T. experiences, Elliott does too. In one scene, for example, E.T. becomes intoxicated on beer and Elliott exhibits the effects at school. E.T. watches a love scene on television between John Wayne and Maureen O'Hara in John Ford's film *The Quiet Man* (1952). At the same time, Elliott, now in science class and under the spell of E.T.'s symbiotic extrasensory perception, quickens his nerve and kisses the prettiest girl in the class. Noticing that his friend E.T. looks like the frogs he and his classmates are about to dissect, Elliott is suddenly compelled to free all the frogs from their glass enclosures, putting himself in trouble with the science teacher.

Elliott finally introduces E.T. to his brother and sister. Gertie is startled when she meets the ugly, but strangely cute, creature whom Elliott has found. She immediately blurts out a scream that alarms E.T.: he cranes his neck up in fear and belches out an unearthly screech. Eventually, Gertie takes an interest in E.T. because he is "someone even smaller than she, an infant brother she can dress up as a bag lady and even teach to speak."[24]

E.T.'s living space is a large closet off Elliott's room filled with clothes, toys, and stuffed animals. It even has a small, multicolored stained glass window, which suggests a spiritual dwelling place for this unusual time traveler. In *E.T.* and *Poltergeist*, the closet becomes the focus of either a hiding place (for E.T.) or a place of terror (in the later film the "TV people" reside there and swallow Carol Ann into the next plane of existence). As Corliss notes, "In a house [Spielberg] had to share with three mischievous younger sisters, Steven would take the standard boy's revenge: lock them in the closet and then throw in the thing they feared most."[25]

For Spielberg, such places seem to represent those special

areas in the suburban home where children feel isolated, yet safe with their thoughts, or, alternately, frightened by images of entrapment or capture by some creature. For a suburban child, these places can be the bathroom, the basement, the attic, or a backyard shed. In all of Spielberg's works to date, there is a sense of such "small places." The sanctuary of the bathroom appears to add the element of spirituality since it contains a source of water, a place to cleanse not only the body but also the soul. Consider, for example, David Mann (*Duel*) splashing water on his face in a roadside café restroom. In *Sugarland Express*, Lou Jean diverts Clovis into a restroom in the minimum security prison. There she has sex with him and unfolds her plan to retrieve Baby Langston. In *Jaws*, the cabin of the *Orca* extends the bathroom motif because it is a small place surrounded by water. The cabin becomes Brody's refuge from the giant killer shark after it devours Quint. He is forced to escape when the shark crashes through the hull filling the small cabin with water. Consider Roy Neary's attempts to cleanse himself of the implanted image in his mind in *Close Encounters*. It is the bathroom where Neary first carves Devil's Tower, out of shaving cream, and where he has his mental breakdown—lying in the bath tub face up, fully clothed, and with the shower on. Indiana Jones's "tight spots" are usually experienced within the confines of insect-ridden, booby-trapped caves, narrow tunnels, or the dark chambers of lost civilizations; his only love scene with Marion commences in the small space of a ship's cabin. The spiritual nature of the cleansing process as rebirth is evident in *Poltergeist*, where mother and daughter are revived and cleansed of the messy afterbirth in a tub of hot water in a downstairs bathroom. When E.T. becomes ill and his life begins to drain from him, he is led into the bathroom with the hope of reviving him and saving him from death. These small places are a natural part of Spielberg's vision because his filmmaking, he says, "comes from some of my experiences growing up."[26] For young Spielberg, these "secret" spaces might have provided him creative refuges from the mundane existence of suburbia, neighborhood bullies, and his three sisters. In *E.T.* and *Poltergeist* the private visual perceptions of a child's world and the many "small places" in it become magnified and focused. The significance of these "small spaces" has grown with each film Spielberg has directed or conceived.

E.T. experiences Halloween with other neighborhood kids (the first time, Spielberg says, E.T. sees other humans), a sequence that is both funny and touching. For E.T.'s disguise, the children dress him up in a sheet, and one of the first "humans" he sees is outfitted in a "Yoda" costume (from Lucas's *Star Wars* series). But unidentified government workers are quietly on the prowl for the little alien. They listen in to neighborhood conversations with ultrasensitive sound equipment, use radiation detectors to pick up traces of the extraterrestrial, and eventually begin a house-to-house inquiry.

Fortunately, E.T. manages to build a transmitter contraption out of spare parts (a Speak n' Spell computer toy, an umbrella, a circular saw blade, bobby pins, and a record player) and places it on a hillside with help from Elliott. While the contraption is bleeping out signals into the heavens, Elliott falls asleep and E.T. stands guard over the machine. He eventually begins to feel ill. He walks off into the forest and when Elliott awakens in the morning, the contraption is still functioning but E.T. is gone! Feeling depressed and ill himself, Elliott walks home to a worried mother, and sends Michael out to find the lost creature. E.T. is found in the forest and brought home. Life has begun to leave E.T., who becomes afraid for Elliott, because his life seems to be draining away too—the result of the symbiotic relationship. The children fetch their mother for help, and it is the first time she sees the ugly creature. Her first thought is to protect her children, and in doing so, attempts to usher them out of the house. When she opens the door, she encounters a man in a space suit. Outside the house, government workers are enveloping the house in a plastic tent to decontaminate it. A makeshift emergency room is set up, and E.T. and Elliott are placed alongside each other on long tables. When E.T. is pricked with a needle, Elliott responds in pain. But E.T.'s life is fading and so is Elliott's. Elliott implores E.T. to heal himself, but he apparently cannot. When it appears hopeless for the extraterrestrial, the doctors turn their attention to saving Elliott. Even that now appears futile.

E.T. dies, but Elliott miraculously comes back to full health. He looks at his dead friend and pleads for him to come back to life, but the alien remains pale and motionless. Later, viewing his friend for the last time, Elliott notices E.T.'s heartlight glowing. Overjoyed that his friend is not dead, he knows he must help E.T. escape the government workers. He gets Michael to recruit his friends for help. Pretending E.T. is still dead, Elliott closes the lead tomblike container and follows it through the plastic tunnel to the waiting van. Once inside, he opens the tomb, brushes away the ice and helps E.T. out. Michael, meanwhile, sneaks into the cab of the van, starts the engine, and zooms off, dragging along the plastic tunnel with the two men still inside it. When the men begin to climb forward, Elliott unfastens the tunnel, dropping the workers in the middle of the road. Michael, although too young to have a license, succeeds in driving the van to the meeting place, where his friends are waiting with bicycles. Elliott places E.T. in his bike's basket and the bikers head for the rendezvous location where E.T.'s spaceship will pick him up. When government workers and police trap the bikers with a roadblock, E.T. miraculously makes the bicycles fly off the ground (in classic Disney style) and past the moon (recalling Peter Pan).

At the rendezvous site, Spielberg indulges in a touching, but overly long, goodbye betwen E.T. and Elliott, while the others—Gertie, Michael, and their mother—look on in wonder and amazement. Gertie gives E.T. a geranium plant that had come back to life, and E.T. tells her to "be good." Then he waddles up the ramp of the ship, the hatch quickly closes, the ship rises. E.T. is finally going home after his adventure on planet Earth.

E.T. is Spielberg's most evenly paced film. For the first time, he allows the characters to set the pace, which is much subdued compared to his other works. The richness of the film lies in its casting. Spielberg's choice for Elliott was important because it reflects his youthful remembrances of himself—intelligent and inquisitive, yet very much alone and far from popular. The role of Elliott went to young Henry Thomas from San Antonio, Texas, who had just finished his first feature film, *Raggedy Man* (1982). His first reading for Spielberg was atrocious, but he won the part when he was asked to improvise.[27]

Cast as the older brother was a more experienced stage actor, Robert MacNaughton, son of Bruce MacNaughton, who, as a child actor himself, played the blond rich kid in Hal Roach's *Little Rascals* series. Drew Barrymore, playing Gertie, comes directly from third-generation cinematic lineage—her grandfather was John Barrymore, the famous actor of the silent era and early sound films. With innocent-looking eyes, blond hair, and a charming pose, she is convincing as the impish young sister, who may be an "amalgamation of [Spielberg's] three 'terrifying' sisters."[28] Before becoming Elliott's sister in *E.T.*, she was featured in several television commercials and a television movie, and appeared as one of Dr. Jessup's daughters in Ken Russell's *Altered States* (1981).

Casting the suburban children was crucial from the start, because they were required to carry much of the film. The adults in this movie (there are only two) appear unimportant and almost invisible. Elliott's mother, Mary (Dee Wallace), knocks over E.T. in the kitchen without ever realizing what he is (another toy perhaps?). When she enters Elliott's closet to fetch a blanket, she does not notice the "goblin" Elliott has stashed there: E.T. neatly fits into the lineup of stuffed animals (purposely positioned by Elliott for camouflage) and goes undetected. In establishing the relationship between mother and children, Spielberg purposely re-creates the typical dilemma faced by a young divorced woman forced into the working world to support her children. This scenario enables Spielberg to establish a natural distance between mother and children that does not appear contrived. Elliott and his siblings could as easily have hidden a puppy in the closet.

As in *Close Encounters*, Spielberg portrays government officials and scientists as cold, calculating, and hostile, although like Lacombe, the scientist in *E.T.*, nicknamed "Keys" (Peter Coyote) for the large, clanking key ring he carries, is sympathetic; he can identify with Elliott and understands the bond between him and the alien. He too, since childhood, has been waiting for his special E.T. friend.

The extraordinary magic of the Spielberg-Mathison story is based on a friendship like no other that exhibits tremendous tenderness and warmth. It is like the popular "boy and a dog" story (Disney's *Old Yeller*, 1957) or a variation on the "odd love story" (George Stevens's *Shane*, 1953).[29] Corliss notes, "Not since the glory days of the Walt Disney Productions—40 years and more ago, when *Fantasia* and *Pinocchio* and *Dumbo* first worked their seductive magic on moviegoers of every age—has a film so acutely evoked the twin senses of everyday wonder and otherworldly awe."[30]

Spielberg claims he put himself on the line with this film because prior to *E.T.*, "I was giving *out*, giving *off* things before I would bring something *in*."[31] He was afraid to show his innermost feelings in his work. Spielberg recalls, "There were feelings I developed in my personal life . . . that I had no place to put."[32] They found a place in *E.T.* and *Poltergeist*. Crawley refers to this 1981 development in Spielberg's life as a "breakout catharsis," a "coming out of the closet (in his case, that's the cutting rooms) and showing off not so much his usual bag of mercurial tricks—see Mom, no hands!—but his heart."[33] For Spielberg, age thirty-three, it was his "suburban psychodrama."

Since Spielberg considers *E.T.* his "personal resurrection," his obvious choice for a location was suburbia: "It's a reality to kids; in suburbia you have to create a kids' world apart from an adult world." Spielberg continues, "What better place to keep a creature from outer space a secret from grown-

ups?"[34] The suburban setting prompted *Commonweal* reviewer Tom O'Brien to note:

> In a famous essay, "The UFO as Religious Symbol," C. G.
> Jung suggested that modern man appropriates machine im-
> ages to his own magical purposes, and turns the stuff of science
> to myth, and religion. No filmmaker does this better than Ste-
> ven Spielberg, a suburban animist with a tinge of
> Manicheanism.
> Watch Spielberg's pizzas, watch his toys, dolls, and train
> sets. In *E.T.*, watch his use of Coors beer and Pez candies. On
> one level, this mass of details explains part of the appeal of his
> films—the lovingly nostalgic recreation of American life, par-
> ticularly suburban life, that engages viewer sympathy, tickles
> humor, and establishes credibility for the weird events about
> to happen. On another level, however, these physical, almost
> palpable recreations of the material world are not the antith-
> esis of Spielberg's interest in the uncanny; rather, their inten-
> sity explains it.[35]

It is audiences' familiarity with suburbia (his audiences are
mostly composed of suburbanites) that allows Spielberg to be
efficient with his story, eliminating much narrative and background material to move the story along at a steady pace
(again showing that his greatest fear is boring his audience).[36]
A lack of exposition, however, creates minor flaws in the
film, preventing the audience from fully comprehending
events. For example, we do not understand that the effects of
gravity on E.T.'s body will eventually cause him to die or that
he needs energy pills for food. His fondness for Reese's Pieces
and beer suggest that he is in no danger of starvation, yet he
begins to discolor and become ill. His sudden turn for the
worse, we surmise, might be his depression at not being able
to get home. Is he grieving himself to death or is there another
reason? William Kotzwinkle's novelization of the screenplay
hints that it is a combination of depression, poor diet, and the
effects of gravity that cause E.T. to wither and die. Although
Elliott pleads with E.T. to heal himself, he says he cannot and
becomes fearful for the children, the willow-creature (Elliott's

mother), and even the world, for he does not know what effect his death might have on Earth (total catastrophe?). Its effects on the "atomic secret" held within E.T.'s heartlight have not been determined. Spielberg urges us to use our imagination here, to fill in the holes, and to keep the faith. Most young viewers readily accept the given premises, since they tend not to view the action critically, rather accepting whatever occurs as necessary.

When E.T. dies, Elliott, whose life appears to be fading too, immediately comes back to life. Then E.T.'s heartlight amazingly begins to glow—he has apparently healed himself, we do not know why or how. E.T.'s miraculous resurrection appears somewhat confusing in the film and contrived in the novel. Kotzwinkle fills the reader in with this oblique explanation:

> A beam of golden light shot through inner space. Historians of the cosmos are divided as to the direction from which it came. It was more ancient than E.T., older than the oldest fossil. There are those who claim it was the healing soul of Earth itself, flickering a single thread of what it knew, as a gesture of diplomacy perhaps, towards its alien visitor.
> *"Don't peek in anymore windows,"* some say it said, and was gone.
> Others say the Earth was doomed and could not save itself, that the saving force had come from a sister planet, to lend a hand in pacifying the dragon of the nuclear force.
> And still others heard:
> *dreeple zoonnnnnnqqqqqqqummmmmmtwrrrdssss*
> Calling from the beyond.
> Whatever it was, it touched E.T.'s healing finger, and caused it to glow.
> He healed himself.[37]

Kotzwinkle also explains why Elliott did not die along with E.T.: "E.T. had found at least one of the formulas he sought, that of a shield, cast behind him as he swooned into death, so the boy could not follow."[38] Such exposition would have been impossible for Spielberg, employing his unusual style of filmmaking, to construct, yet such information appears crucial to explain many such events in the film. E.T.'s inability to speak English clearly made film exposition difficult. Even when he did speak, it was in broken words and garbled phrases that were hard to understand. In Kotzwinkle's novelization, E.T. communicates about his situation (of being stranded), his well-being (the effects of gravity and his lack of energy pills), and his knowledge of humans (the willow-creature and her chidren) through extrasensory perception to plants (he talks to the vegetables in the garden next to the house) and animals (the family dog).

These missing links do not deter from the friendship between Elliott and the alien or the final climax of E.T.'s adventure on Earth—we either take them for granted or let our imaginations fill in the blanks. Spielberg is one of those directors who leads his audience like the captain of a ship or the pilot of an aircraft. Our faith is in his ability to get us to our destination; the details of the flight (engine failure?) or the cruise (icebergs?)—are perhaps best kept from the passengers. Spielberg creates a tension, a nervousness, in the audience, holding our attention while shuttling the story to its conclusion—where his (and the audiences') dreams come true: the tenderness of the human (and alien) heart is revealed. It is truly, as Spielberg would contend, wishing upon a star!

CRITICAL REACTION: <u>E.T.</u> AS RELIGIOUS ALLEGORY

Discovering a religious allegory in *E.T.* has become a popular way of viewing Spielberg's 1982 film. In an interview with Andrew Epstein, Melissa Mathison reveals that during production of the film, she, along with cinematographer Allen Daviau, discovered many similarities between her story of E.T. and that of Christ.[39] Mathison (who was educated in a Catholic school in Hollywood) said she told director Spielberg of their discovery and was given the reply, "I'm Jewish, and I don't want to hear anything about this."[40]

Intentional or not, there are a number of similarities between *E.T.* and the Christian story of a visitor from another realm, sent to save humanity. Al Millar, a professor of biblical literature, notes at least thirty-three parallels between E.T.'s visitation and that of the Christian savior, Jesus. In his pamphlet, *'E.T.'—You're More Than a Movie Star*, he begins his list with the following parallels to Christ:

> "E.T. had a prior extra-terrestrial existence."
> "His early life on earth was 'submerged' or hidden."
> "He came to little children."

The list continues with thirty more plausible parallels, including the final point that, like Christ, "E.T. ascended to his original 'home.'"[41] William Kotzwinkle's novelization of the screenplay lessens some of the biblical parallels, so it is interesting to speculate whether the visual techniques used in the film may have emphasized the similarities. Spielberg's tendency to spiritualize outer space (and extraterrestrials) began with *Close Encounters* and reached new heights with his 1982 effort. Robert Short, however, likens *E.T.* to *2001* and other films in the alien genre, which he contends is based on atheistic humanism. He notes: "Clarke and Kubrick would tell us that *no one* is in charge here. The universe is simply a clocklike, impersonal mechanism, utterly blind and unfeeling and indifferent to people and their problems. No one's in charge. The universe just is. Therefore we can only look to ourselves for help and hope. And of course this is 'human-ism' or the deification of humanity."[42]

Spielberg, like Kubrick and Clarke, merely makes the assumption that we are not alone in the universe and whatever is out there in space is not necessarily hostile to humankind nor something that necessarily approximates the Judeo-Christian concept of God. If certain parallels exist between E.T. and the Christ story, they are not unlike similar religious parallels contained in the many science-fiction works (film or literature) that have been created before. That Mathison was unaware of the parallels until filming began, or that Spielberg would not hear of Christian influence creeping into his work, provides some evidence that science fiction, popular myth, and religion are intertwined.

Tom O'Brien, reviewer for *Commonweal*, claims that Spielberg is like many other science fiction directors in that his "[suburban] animism is complicated by the religious extremism which he shares" with them. "According to their plots, whatever comes out of a spaceship must either save us or destroy us."[43] O'Brien likens Spielberg's *E.T.* to Kubrick's *2001* (1968), Richard Donner's *Superman* (1978), Harry Horner's *Red Planet Mars* (1952), and Robert Wise's *The Day the Earth Stood Still* (1951) in the same "hallowed moral tradition . . . where something or someone Godlike or Christlike saves, or at least renews, humanity—or reaffirms its best impulses."[44] For this reason, O'Brien views Spielberg's suburban fantasy as spiritually defective: "As a mythmaker, however, he shares the defect of other creators of science fiction, not excess but defect of imagination. Their substitute religion is based on an unspiritual premise: something physical is going to save or destroy us, depending on whether the E.T.'s involved are angelic or satanic."[45]

Although salvation *may be* "more uncanny than special effects,"[46] there are valid spiritual parallels, as Millar points out, between Spielberg's *E.T.* and the story of Christ. To dismiss the parallels is, frankly, untenable.

Other critics and reviewers were content to hail *E.T.: The Extra-Terrestrial* as a "masterpiece." It has been compared to classic children's movies from *The Wizard of Oz* (1939) to *Spirit of the Beehive* (Spanish, 1973), as well as to nearly every science-fiction film ever made. Spielberg, himself, likes to bring up references to Frank Capra's *It's a Wonderful Life* (1946) and to think of E.T. as his "Christmas story" (classic films like Capra's often pop up during the holidays).

E.T. captured the popular imagination from Ohio to Tokyo

and, according to *Newsweek's* "Portrait of '82" (27 December 1982), E.T.'s famous line "E.T. phone home" became the most "overworked phrase of the year." It also, of course, became another financial bonanza (E.T. cost only his parts—he couldn't ask for a salary or a star dressing room) for Spielberg and company, achieving even larger box-office records than Spielberg's previous hits.

It will be interesting to follow future reactions to the film. Was it 1982's fad, or will it retain its universal appeal? This appeal distinguishes true film classics—they endure beyond their time and place. Steven Spielberg's "instant" classic needs to stand the test of time.

8 / Tragedy in the Twilight Zone

A car is traveling down a lonely dark highway, while inside two friends sing along with golden oldie tunes on the radio. One suggests they play "Name That Tune." Each takes a turn humming an old tune while the other one tries to guess the title. Finally, the passenger (Dan Aykroyd) tells his friend (Albert Brooks) to pull off the road and turn the lights out. He does, and Aykroyd hums the "Twilight Zone" theme song. He turns his face away from the driver, his friend guesses the tune, and Aykroyd turns back, having become a hideous monster. At this point, graphics (a clock, Einstein's formula $E = mc^2$) from the old television series appear on the screen, accompanied by Rod Serling's eerie voice-over: "You're travelling through another dimension, a dimension of not only sight and sound, but of mind; a journey into a wondrous land whose boundaries are that of the imagination. Next-stop: the Twilight Zone."[1]

Although Spielberg did not specifically mention the *Twilight Zone* project, he is quoted by Crawley as saying that his next film project after *Poltergeist* and *E.T.* "will be a twenty-two minute short."[2] This was the "Kick the Can" segment for a film he was producing: *Twilight Zone: The Movie.* The film contained four segments by different directors (all fans of the old television series) in honor of Rod Serling's famous program (which originated in the late fifties and endured until the mid-sixties). Film critic David Ansen notes: "A good case could be made for Rod Serling's 'The Twilight Zone' as the seminal TV series of its time. Is there a TV-era director whose pop fantasies weren't nurtured in this garden of eerie delights? Now four ex-students . . . pay their respects with *Twilight Zone: The Movie,* an anthology which remakes three of

the original episodes and adds a new one. The 'zone' graduates earn widely mixed marks."[3]

THE SUNNYVALE REST HOME
ENTERS THE TWILIGHT ZONE:
"KICK THE CAN"

Spielberg's story was reworked from a television series
script by George Clayton Johnson. For Spielberg's remake, he
employed Johnson as well as Josh Rogan and Spielberg's
scriptwriter friend Richard Matheson (*Duel*, 1971), who wrote
many of the original *Twilight Zone* teleplays. The "Kick the
Can" story was updated, but still focused on a magical old
man, Mr. Bloom (Scatman Crothers), who appears at the Sunnyvale Rest Home to grant the residents their wish—to be
young again.

The original story by Johnson ended with the old folks becoming children again, and running off to relive their lives.
Only Mr. Conroy (who, despite his skepticism, really wants to
be a child again) remains elderly because he cannot rekindle
the child within himself and believe in the magic that leads
to the childhood transformation. Johnson's original story
came at a time when the "baby-boomers" were coming of age
in the early sixties, a time of increasing emphasis on youth in
American society. To be old, tired, and wrinkled was considered embarrassing because it failed the American ideal of
youthful vitality and good looks.

In the eighties old age is more acceptable—self-acceptance
is the trend. In the updated version Johnson, therefore,
changed the perspective. Mrs. Dempsey, for example, says, "I
didn't really ask to be young again, all I wanted to do was
dance! I can be old and dance"; "School is easy . . . but work
another forty years? Forget it!" says Mr. Weinstein; his wife
injects, "In spite of everything, I'm satisfied with my life the

way it was. We should take one day at a time"; then Mr. Bloom interjects, "In that case, let's all go back to bed. Maybe you could wake up in your old bodies again, but with fresh young minds," suggesting the old adage that you are as young as you feel.[4] Only Mr. Agee, a ladies' man in his youth, wants to remain young in order to experience love again. Mr. Conroy implores Mr. Agee to take him along, but Agee shakes his head and, glancing helplessly at Mr. Bloom, says, "It's too late, Leo [Conroy]. You'll have to stay with yourself."[5] And Mr. Agee quickly disappears from the window's ledge into the world.

It is obvious why the storyline appealed to Spielberg, described many times as a kid in an adult body just having fun making movies. Will Spielberg eventually find himself like Mr. Conroy, with the child inside no longer functional and the magic of his moviemaking lost? Spielberg hopes that he, like Mr. Agee will remain forever young.

David Ansen, in his *Newsweek* review, gave Spielberg a grade of "C" for his effort: "The theme is *echt*-Spielberg, and his technique is as stylish as ever, but here it is pushed dangerously close to self-parody. What was innocent, wondrous and charming in E.T. here looks like an advertisement for innocence, wonder and charm."[6]

It appears that this minor story about the aged would have looked much better on the small screen of television (as was the original) than sprawled on a PanaVision screen with Spielberg's favorite techniques of heavy backlighting and strong diffusion. If Spielberg came "dangerously close" to self-parody, it was because he was working in the wrong medium.

JOE DANTE'S FUN HOUSE

For the third segment, Joe Dante chose Richard Matheson's teleplay "It's a Good Life" (based on a story by Jerome Bixby), produced during the 1961 television season. The story focuses on a young boy (Jeremy Licht) who has devastating powers. Kathleen Quinlan stars as the lost traveler, Helen Foley; William Schallert plays Anthony's father, and veteran actor Kevin McCarthy, Anthony's Uncle Walt. In the original teleplay, Billy Mumy played the part of Anthony, but in Dante's remake, Mumy only makes a guest appearance as a minor character in a diner where his successor to the role plays a video arcade game.

Dante's expressionistic style contributes to the cartoonlike quality of the characters. Those calling themselves Anthony's family are not really his family; the boy has merely adopted them into his bizarre fantasy world where they are at his mercy. In effect, Anthony can will anything he wants, terrorizing those around him. His favorite activity is watching televison, especially cartoons. Anthony creates his fun by willing monstrous cartoon creatures (foreshadowing the "Gremlins" to come) out of the television and into the living room to scare his family half to death. In one scene, he becomes upset with his "sister" and wills her into cartoonland; in another scene, we learn that Anthony has willed the mouth off the face of his other "sister," who listlessly stares at a television set—mouthless—in an upstairs bedroom. Helen perceives Anthony to be a spoiled little boy who only needs love and understanding. After Anthony wishes his family and his fantasy world away, she adopts him and offers to help control his powers. Anthony agrees, but his power is at work again; as Helen and the boy drive down the road, flowers begin to sprout everywhere. Ansen gave Dante a "B" for his effort, noting: "With segment three . . . the movie finally gets spooky. . . . Watching this blackly comic tale . . . is like entering an ominous fun house designed by a mad 10-year-old. It gets a B only because of its weak finale."[7]

"It's a Good Life," however, is only a sample of what Joe Dante did in his next feature film, *Gremlins*, produced by Steven Spielberg in 1984.

GEORGE MILLER'S MINI-REMAKE OF <u>AIRPORT</u>:
"NIGHTMARE AT 20,000 FEET"

The last segment—by far the best—is a remake of the 1964 "Twilight Zone" teleplay, "Nightmare at 20,000 Feet," that starred William Shatner (Captain Kirk of *Star Trek*). Directed by George Miller, the Australian filmmaker noted for his action films in the *Mad Max* series, the movie remake stars John Lithgow as the airplane passenger who believes there is a monster on the wing of the plane.

Good production values, fine performances from Lithgow and Abbe Lane as the stewardess, and a latex monster crafted with all the special effects refinements of the eighties, distinguish Miller's episode. When Lithgow is carried off the plane on a stretcher, Aykroyd and Brooks—the same comedians who opened the film—leer at him in the ambulance, providing a funny ending for the segment and the film.

Miller generates the same suspense and terror as the original, perhaps even more, prompting Ansen to give "an A for this Mad Max of action directors, who leaves his American colleagues biting the dust behind him."[8]

JOHN LANDIS'S TRAGEDY IN THE TWILIGHT ZONE

First things last, in the case of this ill-fated experiment. The first segment, directed by John Landis (who previously directed *The Blues Brothers* [1980] and *American Werewolf In London* [1981]), has an original screenplay written by Landis himself. His story revolves around a disgruntled bigot (Vic Morrow) whose racial slurs encompass blacks, Jews, and Asians. Morrow's character eventually enters the twilight zone and becomes the victim of his own bigotry.

Shooting for this segment began on 1 June 1982; by 23 June filming was almost complete except for one scene, set in Vietnam, that involved Morrow and two young children running from a helicopter. During the shooting, the helicopter crashed on top of Morrow and the two children, killing them as a result. Apparently, the helicopter flew too close to fireball explosions set off by special effect charges. This ripped off the tail section, causing the vehicle to crash. Assistant camera operator Randall Robinson told the newspapers that "the fireballs were much stronger than anyone anticipated."[9]

In the months that followed, many questions about the accident were left unanswered. Landis, associate producer George Folsey, Jr., production manager Dan Allingham, and Warner Brothers were given penalty fines of five thousand dollars by the California Labor Commission for violation of the child labor laws. The children did not possess work permits; they were not members of the Screen Actors' Guild; and they did not have a teacher or welfare worker on the set with them—all required by law.[10]

The incident sparked a drive for more safety codes, especially for those guilds (actors and cameramen) whose members were directly involved in the filming of stunts. Crawley notes that only three months before this tragic accident, a camera crew riding in a helicopter was killed filming special effects sequences for *Birds of Prey II*.[11] By June 1983, almost a year after the accident, John Landis and four associates were indicted by a grand jury on charges of involuntary manslaughter.[12] Crawley notes that special effects driver Carl Pittman stated he saw Spielberg on the set shortly before the accident, but Spielberg denied these charges. In the end, Spielberg was personally cleared of any wrongdoing.

Film critic Ansen said he gave this segment an "F" because Landis "fumbles the opening kick off with a heavy-handed message movie," and the segment's "poor quality and moralizing tone make that tragedy doubly obscene."[13]

As exemplified by Ansen's reactions, *Twilight Zone: The Movie* received mixed reviews from critics and viewers alike. It is not certain how much of the reaction to the film was caused by the tragic incident that almost aborted the film.

Suzanne Harper notes one typical Spielberg fan who did not like the film had "expected more" from the filmmaker.[14] Many of the "Twilight Zone" shows, in fact, were clever teleplays that relied heavily on allegory, metaphor, or character reversal. They were not necessarily action-packed or terror filled, typically Spielberg's trademarks.

It seems only fitting that Spielberg produce a tribute to Rod Serling and his classic television series—he had directed the premier segment for "Night Gallery," a near-resurrection of "The Twilight Zone" also hosted by Rod Serling. The project required catering to older audiences (mid-thirties to forties) of which Spielberg was now a part. Its success depended on the enthusiasm of these older die-hard fans of the original series. Considering the failure of *I Wanna Hold Your Hand* (1978), a film designed for Beatles fans by Spielberg's protégés Robert Zemeckis and Bob Gale, one would think Spielberg might be wary of such a project. The nostalgia craze, which flourished in the early seventies with such films as *The Summer of '42* (1971), *The Last Picture Show* (1971), and *American Graffiti* (1973), seemed to have run its course by the latter part of the decade; hence the poor response to George Lucas's *More American Graffiti* (1979) and the lack of enthusiasm for films like *Flash Gordon* (1980) and *The Lone Ranger* (1981). The only superhero film that was considered a box-office success during the late 1970s was *Superman* (1978). *Twilight Zone: The Movie* was a risk for Spielberg, but one motivated by sincere admiration for one of television's most creative talents—Rod Serling.

9 / "It's a Boy's Life"

After the huge success of *Jaws* and *Close Encounters*, Spielberg had become one of Hollywood's hottest directors. He had always felt that he, along with Lucas, Coppola, and others, would eventually inherit Hollywood. But he was becoming concerned about who would inherit Hollywood from them. "If each studio," says Spielberg, "would take $1 million profit per big movie and invest it in film school and writing programmes, we'd have the industry that David O. Selznick and Irving Thalberg created. It's just silly of the industry not to replenish the well. If they don't look toward the future, who will?"[1]

Both Spielberg and Lucas agree that the Hollywood dream factory needs replenishing and they have taken a number of steps to correct the industry's shortsightedness. One such endeavor is their effort to raise money for the University of Southern California's cinema-television center, a sprawling complex of sound stages, mixing, projection, and editing facilities. In addition, Spielberg has personally helped several former film students get a start in the business. These include Robert Zemeckis and Bob Gale, who graduated from USC (Spielberg produced their initial efforts) and Kevin Reynolds (Spielberg shepherded his short-lived *Fandango* [1985] through production at Warner Brothers).

These were magnanimous gestures on Spielberg's part considering the difficulty of his own entry into the motion-picture business. The small, personal films he made in 16-mm during the 1960s got him nowhere. Studio heads and producers closed their doors on him. Crawley asserts that "it has never been easy to crack the defenses of Hollywood's ruling Establishment," citing Spielberg's age ("he was a sprog") as the main problem.[2]

136

I WANNA HOLD YOUR HAND (1978)
AND USED CARS (1980)
(BEATLEMANIA AND AN AMERICAN TRADITION)

Spielberg's producing efforts began with a script written by the two Bobs, Zemeckis and Gale. According to Crawley, their success story is not unike Spielberg's supposed Universal caper, which gives hope to every filmmaker of gaining entry into Hollywood's dream machine.[3] After seeing *Jaws*, the two Bobs were impressed; they decided to replicate the Spielberg myth by crashing into his office during a tour of Universal Studios.[4] Crawley suggests that this episode was a desperate effort by Zemeckis and Gale to get Spielberg's attention. John Milius had shown interest in two of their scripts, "Tank" and "The Great Los Angeles Air Raid," and had delivered the latter to Metro-Goldwyn-Mayer, but financing never materialized.[5]

According to Crawley, Spielberg was impressed by Zemeckis's student film project, *Field of Honor*, noting the quality and complexity achieved on a shoestring budget.[6] He decided to help them after reading the script for *I Wanna Hold Your Hand* (formerly titled "Beatlemania"). The script was originally taken to Warner Brothers and although the studio was interested, it eventually turned the project down. With another dead end facing them, Spielberg took them over to Universal, where Verna Fields, Spielberg's editor on *Jaws*, had been promoted to a new position: she was now in charge of discovering new talent. With Spielberg behind them, the deal at Universal was sealed for $2.6 million.[7]

The film was about the hysteria of the Beatles's 1964 arrival in America. Although the Beatles themselves were not in the film, Zemeckis edited creatively using old news footage and clips from the "Ed Sullivan Show" on which they appeared in their American television debut. The critics were favorable to the film, but audiences were not enthusiastic. Crawley notes that "the film's opening date, April, 1978, was not February 1964. America's new youth, the children of the flower children thought The Rolling Stones were one of the new-fashioned American soccer sides. They did not, as they say, know from the Beatles. The real fans of John, Paul, George and Ringo were not quite nostalgic enough for the Liverpool sound."[8] The film lost considerable money at the box office, a disappointment to both Zemeckis and Gale. It was not a very propitious start, but with Spielberg's help they had managed to enter the Hollywood dreamscape.

Spielberg supported them again on their second venture, *Used Cars* (1980), a wacky comedy about two brothers who own rival used-car lots across the street from one another. The film featured Zemeckis and Gale's looney brand of comedy tightly edited by one of Spielberg's favorite editors, Michael Kahn. Although the film's direction by Zemeckis was energetic, the one-liners and the throw-away gags become tedious by mid-film. A car sequence, on a smaller scale reminiscent of Spielberg's *Sugarland Express*, was as entertaining as those in *The Gumball Rally* (1976) or *The Cannonball Run* (1981). The critics were split on *Used Cars;* one complained that the film never got beyond its one-joke premise, while another found the film "supercharged."[9] According to Spielberg, "I think the film essentially failed based on concept failure as opposed to failure of writing or execution. I think it is the funniest movie Bob Zemeckis and Bob Gale have ever written, and it just showed what a good director Bob Zemeckis is. For me, it was Bob Zemeckis's rather anti-social, irreverent *American Graffiti*."[10]

Aside from mixed reviews, the film did poorly at the box office. Spielberg summed up the failure as "an American kick reflex to turn the used car commercials off during the late show."[11] This film was yet another failure for Spielberg, his third in the two-year period between 1978 and 1980.

DARK DREAMS:
POLTERGEIST (1982)
(A NEW KIND OF GHOST)

Spielberg now became much more involved in the films that he produced. When he was finishing up post production on *Raiders of the Lost Ark*, he rewrote an original screenplay entitled *Poltergeist*—a collaborative effort with Mark Victor and Michael Grais—to be produced by Frank Marshall, his energetic coproducer. This film represented Spielberg's "dark dreams," while his other film in preproduction, *E.T.: The Extra-Terrestrial*, represented his "nice dreams." Because union rules prevented Spielberg from directing two motion pictures at once, he hired Tobe Hooper as director while he acted as a "line producer" controlling most of the creative decisions involving the film.

This was a new experience for the maturing Spielberg, who usually left his directors alone when acting as executive producer. *Poltergeist*, on the other hand, was Spielberg's creation from the start. Hooper was best known for his *Texas Chainsaw Massacre* (1974), a low-budget slasher film that started a new fad in the late seventies and early eighties (*Halloween*, 1978; *Friday The 13th*, 1980; *Happy Birthday To Me*, 1981). The result of the Spielberg-Hooper collaboration was less than satisfying for Hollywood's wunderkind, who was quoted in a *Rolling Stone* interview as saying, "Well, the turmoil is essentially created by wanting to do it your own way and having to go through procedure. That is why I will never again *not* direct a film I write."[12] Although the film is credited to director Hooper, *Poltergeist* clearly exhibits Spielberg's creative directorial input, style, and subtle wit. Several clips of "behind-the-scenes" action focus on Spielberg directing JoBeth Williams and Heather O'Rourke as they fall through a ceiling, as well as the scene involving Williams in the swimming pool with skeletons. Spielberg's active participation in the film was apparently due to Hooper's willingness to cooperate.

Spielberg notes, "It was frustrating for Tobe Hooper, and it was frustrating for the actors, who were pretty torn between my presence and his on the set every day. But rather than Tobe's saying, 'I can't stand it. Go to Hawaii, get off the set,' he'd laugh and I'd laugh. If he'd said, 'I've got some ideas that you're not letting into this movie, I would love you to see dailies, consult, but don't be on the set,' I probably would have left."[13]

Despite these confusions, the film was a highly creative contemporary horror tale. Written by Spielberg himself, the story takes place in his favorite setting—a sprawling suburban subdivision where every house looks the same and where Steve Freeling (Craig T. Nelson), a somber, real-estate developer in his mid-thirties, lives with his youthful wife (JoBeth Williams) and three children. Spielberg's basic premise was to focus not on old-fashioned ghosts, but on poltergeists, noisy ghosts who are spirits of the dead trapped in limbo above the earth before they can cross over into the "light."

Spielberg did not have to venture far to discover his ghost story. As Crawley notes suspiciously:

> *Poltergeist* stems from the fall-out from dumping the *After School* and *Night Skies* projects; and so, for that matter does *E.T.* It is as if he put both rejects through a screenplay-mincer and used the main extract as the basis for new films [*sic*] menus.... *After School* ... was about suburban kids, what else; it always had been, even when it was *Growing Up. Night Skies* had a farm-house invaded by aliens. Right, okay ... turn the aliens into spectres and put the invaded home in suburbia and put three kids in it. They are almost neighbours of the *E.T.* brood, for whom he retained the aliens.[14]

Spielberg claimed to have written the screenplay in five days, dubbing it a "stream of consciousness movie," but Crawley notes that the result was "low on depth of character, higher on special effects."[15] His characterization has the effect, however, of making the figures into "everyman" and "everywoman." The *Poltergeist* screenplay shows Spielberg's plotting and characterization clearly since this work is not an adaptation—like *Jaws* where he (and Carl Gottlieb) imposed a three-act structure and one-dimensional characters on Peter Benchley's multiple plot-line. That Spielberg prefers strong but one-dimensional characters reflects his concept of film entertainment: omitting laborious character development, he allows the action to dominate and hold viewers' attention. One can surmise that as a child Spielberg was bored by films—such as war or action-adventure films—where critical action pauses for character development or a love scene, both of which are very much absent in his films. Because Spielberg's films are visually captivating and devoid of "pauses" that break the action, they resemble television programs where shots between commercial breaks do not run beyond five seconds before a cut or dissolve is made. Spielberg's "action" is clearly tailor-made for TV-generation viewers.

Spielberg's characters are usually suburban types very much like the suburban moviegoers sitting in shopping mall theaters watching them. Because of an assumed identification, much of the character depth is established in the opening scenes. During the bedroom scene in *Poltergeist*, for example, Steve reads a book aptly titled *Reagan: The President, the Man*, while his wife, Diane, rolls a marijuana cigarette. From this scenario, we may speculate that Diane, an earthy, sassy type, was possibly involved with liberal sixties activity in college (her daughter Dana, remember, is a teenager), while Steve was probably the conservative onlooker more concerned with his studies. They are clearly "baby boomers" of the peace generation who have graduated to the comforts and luxury of middle-class suburban life.

The plot of *Poltergeist* is a conventional ghost story elevated by the uniqueness of the characters and visually enhanced by the innovative special effects supplied by George Lucas's Industrial Light and Magic team. The film opens with an extreme close-up shot of a Sony television set. The television station is signing off with the national anthem as Spielberg's camera pulls back to reveal the electronic image. When the anthem is over, the station turns off its carrier signal, leaving only video interference and crackle. All are asleep except the family dog, who is using the opportunity to scout for midnight snacks. Then, the child Carol Ann is awakened. Still somewhat dazed, she walks downstairs, sits in front of the imageless set, and begins having what appears to be a one-way conversation with the television, asking questions like "Who are you" and "Where do you come from?" Only Carol Ann can hear the replies; the viewer remains unilluminated as to the nature of the "TV people" (as Carol Ann refers to them later in the film). Thus begins the reign of terror in the Freeling household.

The film should end when, through the aid of a psychic (Zelda Rubenstein) brought in by Dr. Lesh, the parapsychologist, Carol Ann is retrieved via the "bilocation" (reentry) point and the psychic declares the house free of spirits. But Spielberg does not stop his story here. The film contains a double climax; in the second part Spielberg-Hooper unleash the potent special effects supervised by Richard Edlund and mechanical effects created by Mike Woods (who also assisted Spielberg on *Jaws* and *Close Encounters*). A giant esophagus appears from the children's closet and attempts to swallow Carol Ann while a clown doll (an object Spielberg claims was his "biggest fear" in childhood)[16] comes to life and tries to strangle Robbie. Diane is blocked from her children by an eerie creature who stands guard outside the bedroom. Coffins erupt from the ground, skeletons float in the pool, and the disruption spreads panic and confusion throughout the subdivision. After the Freelings escape from their house, it implodes, disappearing into another dimension.

This ending, although a surprise, disrupts the pacing of the film for die-hard horror fans expecting a ghoulish finish; it appears tacked on. Crawley notes that this part of the film is "clearly unSpielbergian" and "wholly Hooperish." The sequence "also happens to be Spielberg's least favourite part of the film."[17] In the final scene, the Freelings drive to the local Holiday Inn, where they check in for the night. In Spielberg's final statement about television (he's a television junkie), Steve Freeling rolls the set out of the motel room into the rain and returns to the motel room slamming the door behind him. There is no commercial here, just "the end."

CONTEMPORARY TERROR IN SUBURBIA:
GREMLINS (1984)
(E.T. TURNS INTO A DEVIL AFTER MIDNIGHT)

Two years after *E.T.* and *Poltergeist,* Spielberg tried a double release again with *Temple of Doom* and *Gremlins,* but this time the less promoted film (which Spielberg had left to another director, Joe Dante) almost overshadowed the much publicized prequel to *Raiders of the Lost Ark.* Spielberg's association with Dante grew out of their mutual interest in the "Twilight Zone" television series. Dante directed the third segment, "It's a Good Life," for Spielberg in *Twilight Zone: The Movie* immediately before *Gremlins.* If Dante has one peculiarity, it is that his characters assume a sort of expressionistic quality that can be best described as cartoonlike. This was evident in the *Twilight Zone* segment, but he carried it to new heights in *Gremlins.*

The story involves the purchase of a Mogwai ("who is E.T. and Yoda rolled into a koala bear")[18] by Mr. Peltzer (Hoyt Axton) from an old Chinese gentleman who runs a gift shop in the middle of Chinatown. The Mogwai is a gift for the man's son, Billy (Zach Galligan). Before Mr. Peltzer leaves the shop, the shopkeeper warns that there are three things that one should never do: expose the Mogwai to light (they scream and screech and eventually die from bright light), get them wet (they reproduce six- or sevenfold), and above all "no matter how much they cry, no matter how much they beg, never, *never* feed them after midnight" (they turn into nasty little monsters called gremlins!). Mr. Peltzer heeds the warning and leaves the shop with the Mogwai carefully placed in its box.

Much of what happens from this point onward is predictable—some of it is heartwarming, some comic, and some violent. The Mogwai, a mechanical creature thought up by Hollywood special effects person Chris Walas, is a cute, lovable little thing that is furry all over and has big floppy ears and clear, bright eyes. At first, it is as docile as any adorable pet. We feel sorry for it when it screams because Billy has exposed it to light. When Billy accidentally spills water on it we are amazed to see the result: the Mogwai (called Gizmo) sprouts little puff balls that eventually grow into other Mogwais. But the offspring look a bit more sinister and devilish. Billy gives one to his teacher for observation. Late at night, the caged Mogwai offspring manages to get something to eat—after midnight—and turns into a vicious-looking gremlin. Other Mogwai offspring begin eating after midnight, too, either as a result of careless adults or children feeding them or because they have escaped their cages and are eating on their own. Soon the town is filled with gremlins and havoc breaks loose. In his review David Ansen draws several interesting parallels to other films. "One person calls it 'E.T. with teeth.' You could also say it's 'The Texas Chainsaw Massacre' with Muppets. Then again, it's also 'Invasion of the Body Snatchers' set in a back lot town of Frank Capra's 'It's a Wonderful Life.' In fact, for all the hundreds of movie references one could conjure up to describe this film, no one is likely to confuse *Gremlins* with any other movie."[19]

The film exhibits a "wacky sense of comic horror," which Ansen says "is uniquely its own."[10] The comic scenes show the gremlins as devilish pranksters looking for a good time. The local bar becomes filled with them getting drunk, playing pool, and smashing the place up. The disasters the gremlins create in the small town are fun to watch.

The more violent episodes involve Billy's mother, Mrs. Peltzer (Frances Lee McCain), attempting to rid her kitchen of the gremlins ("In the best of Dante's scenes . . . you may find yourself doubled over with a unique combination of hilarity, nausea and disbelief").[21] She finally traps one in her Mix-Master and liquidates it; green goop spills everywhere. The gremlins are not averse to defending themselves, either: one kills Billy's teacher, and Stripe, the gremlin leader, almost kills Billy. The gremlins also kill a cantankerous old lady by short-circuiting her chairlift, thus propelling her through the air and out the window of her multistory house. "These are the gremlins, nasty devil dolls who will chew their way into your heart."[22]

Eventually the humans prevail, since the gremlins are finally exposed to sunlight. The lesson of responsibility is learned and the Mogwai is taken back by the Chinese shopkeeper. The moral of the story, as the old Chinese man explains, is that "society without responsibility is a society without hope." The lovable Mogwai, Gizmo, and the "morality play" atmosphere are pure Spielberg (derived from Disney).

Like *Temple of Doom*, the film came under attack for its gore and violence, leading to the adoption of the new rating code, PG-13. Yet, despite all the fuss, David Ansen suggests in his *Newsweek* film review: "'Gremlins' is sure to arouse outrage in some circles over its gleeful carnage. But 'Gremlins's' violence, always spiked with wit, will probably be better understood by kids than by their parents. The movie's a demonic toyshop, in which Ken and Barbie grow fangs and turn into juvenile delinquents; what may be disturbing to parents is that kids will identify both with the clean-cut hero and his family *and* the gremlins."[13] *Gremlins* marks Spielberg's first successful film as executive producer, although he did not exercise as much control as he did with *Poltergeist*.

A BUSY 1985

In 1985, Steven Spielberg's professional and personal efforts (he became a father for the first time at thirty-seven) earned him a cover story in *Time*.[24] *Gremlins*'s success had encouraged him to rerelease *E.T.*—the biggest money-maker in movie history—but two other films also appeared in the summer of 1985 under Spielberg's aegis.

Released in June, *The Goonies* (billed as "Steven Spielberg's *The Goonies*," but directed by Richard Donner—con-
tradicting Spielberg's earlier statement that he would "never
again *not* direct a film he wrote") was a commercial and
critical success. Spielberg is credited with original story con-
ception and with executive production (along with Frank
Marshall and Kathleen Kennedy). Chris Columbus's screenplay exhibits many of the hallmarks of Spielberg's work, and
the studio was careful to announce at a press conference that
Spielberg had been closely involved in every stage of production. Richard Corliss quotes Donner as saying, "Steven is over
your shoulder the whole time. He always bows to you because
you're the director, but he's got so many good ideas that you
want to grab every one of them."[25]

The Goonies is fast paced and action filled, causing inevitable comparisons to the Indiana Jones films. But the similarities are only in these areas. *Goonies* is aimed squarely at
the under-13 crowd, as evidenced by its PG (rather than the
new PG-13) rating, and lacks the violence and intensity of the
earlier films.

The film's stars—the Goonies—are a gang of children on a
hunt for pirate treasure. They are accompanied by three older
teenagers, but the film always belongs to the kids. The group
inevitably calls forth comparisons to Hal Roach's "Our
Gang." Leonard Maltin, movie reviewer for the television
show "Entertainment Tonight," cites a clip from "Mama's Little Pirate," a 1934 episode of *The Little Rascals*, that closely
parallels one scene in *Goonies*.[26] It features a comic, fat character named Chunk (Jeff B. Cohen), a smart aleck Alfalfa type
named Mouth (Corey Feldman), an Oriental whiz kid, (played
by the talented young actor from *Temple of Doom*, Ke Huy
Quan), and a sweet, heroic leader named Mikey (Sean Austin),
a Henry Thomas look-a-like.

The loosely conceived plot and the kids' characterizations
are set up in the opening scenes, which many critics fault for
tediousness and lack of clarity. The kids and the problem they

must overcome are introduced at Mikey's house, interestingly located on the side of a hill near the Pacific coast in the small town of Astoria (it is a community that *Newsweek* film reviewer Jack Kroll notes is an "inspired variation on Spielberg's recurring theme of suburbia").[27] Greedy developers are planning to evict the kids and their parents from their homes and the Goonies decide to take action. This resolve leads them to Mikey's attic and to a pirate treasure map. From here on it is the type of thrilling adventures dear to children since Robert Louis Stevenson wrote *Treasure Island*.

Their treasure hunt takes the Goonies to an abandoned restaurant on a coastal hillside by a lighthouse. There they encounter ominous villains (a humorously villainous mother—played by Anne Ramsey—and her two criminal sons, one of whom escaped from the local jail in the film's opening sequence), a dead body, and a friendly, yet hideous giant monster, Sloth (kept chained in the basement by the villains and rescued by Chunk). Wending their way through underground caves, waterfalls, and pools, the kids finally reach a hidden pirate ship replete with skeletons and gaudy treasure.

As in other films, Spielberg here imbeds references to his own and his friends' productions, as well as to classics. *The Goonies* includes a nod to *Gremlins*—in one scene, the sheriff asks Chunk if he is seeing gremlins—and to Spielberg's childhood—one of the girls playing the skeletal organ announces that it is not exactly like playing her mother's Steinway, a reference to Spielberg's mother and her Steinway in the living room of their suburban Phoenix home. Finally, there is an obvious reference to Spielberg himself: when Chunk is spilling his confession to the Fratellis, he recounts an episode where he pretended to vomit on an audience from the balcony of a movie theater, a prank that Spielberg executed in his youth.

The film has a certain mechanical quality because the action is so fast paced. Dialogue is often neglected in favor of action, which is achieved through constant motion and sound (the kids speak constantly and all at once). The action scenes in the underground cave resemble those in *Temple of Doom* and *Raiders* and include a waterslide, which was filmed in a real amusement park ride. *The Goonies* prompted Kroll to write that "Steven Spielberg has become the General Motors of kid's movies."[28]

It is not a major Spielberg film, but it won praise for its fun-filled adventures and good-natured humor. The kids are not fully predictable characterizations and the villains (inspired by the classic characters of *Arsenic and Old Lace*, 1944) are truly delightful. *The Goonies* has an important ingredient lacking in *Temple of Doom* and *Gremlins*—a return to Spielberg's own special identification with childhood and the humanity of his best work.

The summer of 1985 saw yet another Spielberg film, *Back to the Future*, which teamed up once again the two Bobs—Robert Zemeckis and Bob Gale. Zemeckis, who broke away from the team temporarily to direct *Romancing the Stone* (a contemporary comedy adventure in the spirit of the Indiana Jones films), directed this tall tale about a young man named Marty (Michael J. Fox from the television series "Family Ties"), who is thrust back in time where he meets his parents as teenagers. It is played for fun in the same spirit as the previous Zemeckis-Gale enterprise, *Used Cars* (1980).

Marty is a with-it, upbeat high school student who comes from a screwball family and is friends with an eccentric scientist-inventor named Dr. Brown (played by Christopher Lloyd). Dr. Brown's latest invention is a time-traveling, plutonium-powered DeLorean car. The time traveler is Marty, who lands in his hometown—in 1955. The fun begins when Marty discovers that his father is not only a nerdish teenager afraid of local bullies but also a peeping tom. To make matters worse, his mother (who has not met his father yet) develops a puppy-love crush on *him*. Marty realizes that his intrusion into the past is changing the future when he discovers that he and his siblings are fading from a family picture he has in his wallet. In an attempt to order the future properly, Marty engages in a series of bumbling tactics to bring his father and mother together, so that he and his siblings may be conceived. His wacky friend, Dr. Brown, is on hand in the past, too, thirty years younger. In the end, Marty successfully gets his parents together long enough for them to fall in love, and his scientist friend helps him get back to 1985. The premise is farfetched, but exhibits good humor and Disney-like verve.

In *Back to the Future*, Zemeckis parodies Spielberg's suburbanites with the McFly family. Before Marty's time travel, the McFlys are depicted as losers, living in a tiny boxlike house on a street of similar houses. The decor is high-camp tacky and the family is garbed in polyester. Mr. McFly is a wimp, Mrs. McFly an overweight boozer, and Marty's brother (a fast-food employee) and sister are just like their parents. Only Marty is different and he manages to change the course of his family's lives through his time travels. Richard Corliss notes in a review that "the child of 1985 must teach his parents (the children of 1955) how to be cool, successful and loved."[29] But when he does, the McFlys are transformed into a parody of 1980s suburbanites. This form of parody is one Zemeckis handles well. Reportedly, Spielberg lent his support during filming but gave director Zemeckis full reign, sustaining faith in his friend's humor, despite *1941*.

It is not surprising that by the summer of 1985, Spielberg had firmly established himself as a producer; the marquees read "Steven Spielberg's *The Goonies*," and "Steven Spielberg's *Back to the Future*." His power as one of Hollywood's most influential producers had culminated with the release of his blockbuster films *E.T.* and *Poltergeist* in 1982, and the enormous success of the Indiana Jones films with George Lucas. Only a few years previously, Spielberg the producer lacked name recognition, as seen in films like *I Wanna Hold Your Hand* (1978) or *Used Cars* (1980), much less the "name only" credit on *Continental Divide* (1981), a film he withdrew from. It is anticipated that future Spielberg productions will highlight his name, even when prominent directors are at the helm, to ensure the film's success and to carry on the Spielberg legend.

By fall, the network television audience was introduced to yet another Spielberg venture, an anthology entitled "Amazing Stories," which premiered 28 September on NBC. The series is, in Spielberg's words, a "potpourri" of "mini-films," unified by Spielberg's name and high production values. Spielberg says the stories, based on the *Amazing Tales* series that started in 1926 and is now owned by Universal Studios, "were the sort told to me when I was sitting on my father's knee at 4 or 5 years old."[30] As with most of his projects, Spielberg immersed himself completely, writing and directing several of the episodes, including the opening show, "Ghost Train," which featured a train crashing through the walls of a rural home and into the family kitchen.

"Ghost Train" is recognizably Spielberg with its fast-paced dialogue and action, bright backlighting, and score by John Williams. As with his "Kick the Can" segment, Spielberg opts for "nice." It is a touching and slightly haunting story of a grandfather who comes to visit his grandson. As the story progresses, we learn that the grandfather has come to meet death after his long life. As a young boy, the grandfather fell asleep on railroad tracks waiting for a train. He awoke to the sound of locked brakes of the oncoming train, escaping death by jumping out of the way, but causing a tragic train wreck. The man tells his grandson that the train, after all these years, is coming for him, and proudly displays the faded ticket he bought the night of the tragedy. The boy's parents think the old man is imagining things and call for the doctor, who puts him to bed with a sedative. That night, however, the grandson awakes to the sound and motion of a train shaking the house, its single headlight beaming through his bedroom window. The boy runs to fetch his grandfather, who collects everyone in the house and puts them in a "safe" spot. (In an earlier scene, the grandfather deduces that a portion of the house was built over the old railroad line.)

Spielberg makes fantasy comes true when a full-sized train

comes crashing through the house and stops to pickup the grandfather. We assume death has come to the old man when he tells his grandson he cannot go with him, subtly indicating that this will be the last time the family will see him. The episode ends on a light note as the train pulls away with the boy's mother surveying the damage to the house and wondering who their insurance agent is.

With its early Sunday night slot, "Amazing Stories" is clearly aimed at younger viewers. Spielberg's plans, however, include airing episodes not suitable for young children at later viewing times and on other days of the week. This is all part of a unique deal with NBC that also included episode budgets of up to one million dollars each and a guaranteed series run of two seasons. Spielberg's line-up of "television" directors for the other episodes is unusual; included are such accomplished and successful feature-film directors as Martin Scorsese (*Alice Doesn't Live Here Anymore*, 1975; *Taxi Driver*, 1976); Peter Hyams (*Outland*, 1981; and *2010*, 1984), Paul Bartel (*Eating Raoul*, 1984), and Clint Eastwood (*Play Misty for Me*, 1971; *The Eiger Sanction*, 1975). For Spielberg, "Amazing Stories" returns full circle to his roots, when he started out as a journeyman at Universal directing veteran actress Joan Crawford in "*Night Gallery*."

For this energetic filmmaker approaching his forties, the future looks bright. His many projects include two releases as producer—*Young Sherlock Holmes* and *The Money Pit*—and a film version of Alice Walker's Pulitzer Prize–winning novel, *The Color Purple*, which Spielberg began filming in June 1985. This is a major departure for Spielberg, for Walker's story deals with a young black woman's emotional growth and sexual experiences. According to Richard Corliss, "It did not seem the sort of material Steven Spielberg would touch with a ten-foot wand. Which is precisely why he went for it." Corliss quotes Spielberg as saying, "*The Color Purple* is the biggest challenge of my career."[31]

A major part of Spielberg's challenge was translating into

film the epistolary technique of Alice Walker's novel. In the book, the story is told entirely through the letters that the heroine, Celie, writes to God and those she receives from her sister, Nettie. It is through these letters that Walker reveals the remarkable psychological growth of Celie, detailing her struggles in a trap of male domination and violence in turn-of-the-century Georgia and her eventual realization of her place in the universe and her needs for love and personal fulfillment. Scriptwriter Menno Meyjes apparently structured enough chronological events from the letters to tempt Spielberg's interest in bringing such a noted literary work to the silver screen.

For Spielberg to attempt this film is in itself praiseworthy. Considering his preference for linear storylines with lots of action, one would think that an epistolary novel without a clearly defined plot would have seemed totally unworkable. Critics are ambivalent as to whether or not Spielberg succeeds with *The Color Purple*'s adaptation to the screen. A review in *Daily Variety* claims, "There are some great scenes and great performances in 'The Color Purple,' but it is not a great film," and that "comparisons to Walker's best-selling novel are inevitable and it seems safe to say that those who haven't read the book will be more favorably disposed to the film."[32]

The problems stem from translating first-person point of view to that of the camera, which in Spielberg's film can only be an observer. In the transformation from the novel to the screen the point of view of the story shifts. The focus and overall feeling in the first part of the novel lie totally within the realm of Celie's perspective. By contrast, the film's point of view operates externally and quite independently of Celie or her feelings. Up until the time she breaks out of her oppression (about two-thirds of the way into the film), Celie (played by Whoopi Goldberg) is overshadowed, for the most part, by more colorful characters. The change of perspective, although necessary in film, is probably why her transformation seems rather abrupt and contrived. During this part of the film, however, the audience is allowed to see and finally understand Celie. Spielberg keeps us as unaware as Celie is supposed to be up to this point, a technique perhaps misunderstood by some reviewers who always want an absolutely literal adaptation of any novel. Here, Spielberg allows us glimpses of Celie's perspective when she, over a short but intense period of time, feverishly reads all of Nettie's letters (dating back more than twenty years), which Celie's husband—known to her only as Mr.—had hidden since the day he ran Nettie off.

With her lost sister and her two children found again, and her awareness of her lesbian love for Shug Avery (merely touched upon in the film, but an important aspect of the novel), Celie takes command of her life, perhaps without enough psychological development of her character to make her transformation really credible. Again, Spielberg relies on the visual to fill in any missing pieces, causing Richard Corliss to comment that "Spielberg has chosen to elegize the story by romanticising it, swathing the characters in Norman Rockwell attitudes, a meddlesome symphonic score and a golden fairy dust that shines through the windows like God's blessing."[33] This technique perhaps worked better in *E.T.: The Extra-Terrestrial* because that was essentially an adventure-fantasy film where anything could happen and where many of the loopholes, gaps, or confusions could be filled in by the imagination. It does cause some problems with *The Color Purple*, but Spielberg captures an essential optimism and value for humanity that is an important part of Walker's work as well as his own. According to Thadious Davis, writing about the novel, Celie's affirmation of herself when she says "I'm pore, I'm black, I may be ugly and can't cook, a voice say to everything listening. But I'm here"[34] is "Celie's verbal connection to [Langston] Hughes's black everyman and the black oral tradition extends her affirmation of self, so that it becomes racial, as well as personal. . . . Her act of writing and affirming is magnificient. It is an achievement deserving of celebration."[35] Spielberg's movie extends and enhances Walker's novel by re-creating this sense of celebration. He translates Walker's art into the more popularly accessible medium of film.

Through memorable performances and a talented film crew (the cinematography was provided by Allen Daviau, who filmed *E.T.*), Spielberg has created a film that should please moviegoing audiences (always his first concern) and also expand interest in Alice Walker's novel, which deserves a wider audience. The film captured eleven Academy Award nominations, including Best Picture of the Year, but, as was the situation with *Jaws* exactly ten years before, Spielberg was not nominated for Best Director.

Spielberg's title as the "General Motors of kid movies" is well deserved, but one can only wait and see what success, if any, films with more adult themes will bring him. In the summer of 1985, Spielberg fathered his first child, Max Samuel, with actress Amy Irving, suggesting that he is entering a new phase of his personal life, as well as a new phase in his career. If the next ten years are as successful as the last ten, he will certainly be immortalized as one of the most enduring and influential directors in Hollywood history.

Notes and References

Chapter 1

1. Pauline Kael, "Notes on Evolving Heroes, Morals, Audiences," in *When the Lights Go Down* (New York: Holt, Rinehart and Winston, 1980), 195, reprinted from *New Yorker*, 8 November 1976; I. C. Jarvie, *Movies as Social Criticism: Aspects of Their Social Psychology* (Metuchen, N.J.: Scarecrow Press, 1978), 98.

2. Michael Pye and Linda Myles, *The Movie Brats* (New York, 1979), 236–37, 240.

3. Seth Cagin and Philip Dray, *Hollywood Films of the Seventies: Sex, Drugs, Violence, Rock 'n' Roll and Politics* (New York: Harper and Row, 1984), xiv.

4. Dale Pollock, *Skywalking: The Life and Films of George Lucas* (New York: Harmony Books, 1983), 34–35, 42.

5. Charles Moritz, ed., *Current Biography Yearbook 1978* (New York: H. W. Wilson, 1978), 401. Spielberg is quoted by Suzanne Harper as saying, "I didn't quite finish college; when I was a junior, Sid Sheinberg, who's now president of Universal and was at that time head of television for Universal, saw a short film I'd made in school and hired me to direct professionally. So I began directing a year shy of graduation which my father will *never* forgive me for" ("Spielberg," *Nutshell: The Magazine for the College Community*, Spring 1984, 52.).

6. See Jerzy Toeplitz's excellent discussion in *Hollywood and After: The Changing Face of Movies in America*, trans. Boleslaw Sulik (Chicago: Henry Regnery Co., 1975), 90, 251.

7. Michael Sragow, "A Conversation with Steven Spielberg," *Rolling Stone*, 22 July 1982, 28.

8. Carl Gottlieb, *The Jaws Log* (New York, 1975), 24.

9. Pauline Kael, "Sugarland and Badlands," in *Reeling* (Boston and Toronto: Little, Brown & Co.), 300.

10. Pauline Kael, "The Greening of the Solar System," in *When the Lights Go Down*, 348, reprinted from *New Yorker*, 28 November 1977.

11. Jean-Pierre Coursodon with Pierre Sâuvage, *American Directors, Vol. II* (New York, 1983), 343.

12. Todd McCarthy, "Sand Castles," *Film Comment* 18, no. 3 (May–June 1982):53.

13. Dick Cavett, Interview, PBS. Originally produced by WNET-TV, New York. 17 June 1981.

14. Derek Taylor, *The Making of "Raiders of the Lost Ark"* (New York, 1981), 97.

15. Sragow, "Conversation," 25.

16. Taylor, *Making of "Raiders,"* 97.

17. Steve Fox, "20/20" interview, ABC-TV, 24 June 1982.

18. Moritz, ed., *Current Biography Yearbook 1978*, 401.

19. Fox, "20/20" interview, 24 June 1982.

20. David Hartman, Interview with Leah Adler, "Good Morning America," ABC-TV, 5 May 1983.

21. Moritz, ed., *Current Biography Yearbook 1978*, 400–401.

22. Ibid., 400–401.

23. Susan Royal, "Steven Spielberg: In His Adventures on Earth," *American Premiere*, 20 July 1982, 24.

24. Fox, *20/20* interview, 24 June 1982.

25. Sragow, "Conversation," 26.

26. Kael, "Greening," 353.

27. Pye and Myles, *Movie Brats*, 231.

28. Sragow, "Conversation," 25–26.

29. Julian Smith, *Chaplin* (Boston: Twayne, 1984), 146.

30. Hartman, Interview with Leah Adler.

31. Pye and Myles, *Movie Brats*, 24.

32. Sragow, "Conversation," 26.

33. Jarvie, *Movies as Social Criticism*, 96.

34. Moritz, ed., *Current Biography Yearbook 1978*, 401.

35. See, for example, Spielberg, "Directing *1941*," *American Cinematographer* 60, no. 12 (December 1979):1212–15, 1251, 1258, 1259, 1275–76.

36. Fox, *20/20* interview, 24 June 1982.

37. Jack Kroll, "Close Encounter with Spielberg," *Newsweek*, 21 November 1977, 98.

38. David Reiss, "*Raiders of the Lost Ark*: An Interview with Steve Spielberg," *Filmmakers Monthly* 14, no. 9/10 (July–August 1981):32.

39. Royal, "Steven Spielberg," 19.

40. Alan Arkush, "I Remember Film School," *Film Comment* 19, no. 6 (November-December 1983):57.

41. Lev Kuleshov, "The Principles of Montage," in *Kuleshov on Film: Writings of Lev Kuleshov*, trans. and ed. with an introduction by Ronald Levaco (Berkeley: University of California Press, 1974), 183–95; for a discussion of backlighting, see Lev Kuleshov, "Art of the Cinema," *Kuleshov on Film*, 83.

42. Toeplitz, *Hollywood and After*, 92.

Chapter 2

1. Mitch Tuchman, "Close Encounter with Steven Spielberg," *Film Comment* 14, no. 1 (January–February 1978):51.
2. Ibid., 52.
3. Ibid., 52–53.
4. Ibid., 53.
5. Pye and Myles, *Movie Brats*, 223.
6. Ibid., 224.
7. Ibid., 225.
8. Ibid., 224.
9. Ibid., 227.
10. Tuchman, "Close Encounter," 53.
11. Ibid., 53.
12. Pye and Myles, *Movie Brats*, 228.
13. Ibid., 228.
14. Pye and Myles, *Movie Brats*, 227–28.
15. Paul Zimmerman, "Hard Riders," *Newsweek*, 8 April 1974, 82.
16. Ibid., 82.
17. Tony Crawley, *The Steven Spielberg Story: The Man behind the Movies* (New York, 1983), 35.
18. Tuchman, "Close Encounter," 53.
19. Zimmerman, "Hard Riders," 82.
20. Royal, "Steven Spielberg," 20.
21. Pye and Myles, *Movie Brats*, 230.
22. Alvin Marill, "Film Reviews: *Sugarland Express,*" *Films in Review*, 25, no. 5 (May 1974):308.
23. Gottlieb, *Jaws Log*, 52.

Chapter 3

1. Gottlieb, *Jaws Log*, 24.
2. "Summer of the Shark," *Time*, 23 June 1975, 44.
3. Gottlieb, *Jaws Log*, 24.
4. Ibid., 28, 23.
5. Gottlieb, *Jaws Log*, 25.
6. Frank Rich, "The Aliens are Coming," *Time*, 7 November 1977, 102.
7. "Summer of the Shark," 43.
8. "Summer of the Shark," 43; Gottlieb, *Jaws Log*, 54.
9. "Summer of the Shark," 43. Pye and Myles also claim that Milius was involved though not credited in the writing of a version of the screenplay, *Movie Brats*, 171.

10. Gottlieb, *Jaws Log*, 51 ff.

11. Gottlieb, *Jaws Log*, 60.

12. "Summer of the Shark," 42.

13. Arthur Cooper, "The Naked Tooth," *Newsweek*, 23 June 1975, 54; see Gottlieb, *Jaws Log*, 152, for a discussion of the *Newsweek* article.

14. William Goldman, *Adventures in the Screen Trade: A Personal View of Hollywood and Screenwriting* (New York: Warner Books, 1983), 324.

15. Ibid., 324.

16. Gottlieb, *Jaws Log*, 28.

17. Dick Cavett, Interview, 2 July 1981.

18. Gottlieb, *Jaws Log*, 46.

19. "Summer of the Shark," 49.

20. Ibid., 49.

21. Gottlieb, *Jaws Log*, 66.

22. Ibid., 48–49.

23. Cooper, "Naked Tooth," 54.

24. "Summer of the Shark," 50.

25. François Truffaut, Foreword, in Andre Bazin's *Orson Welles: A Critical View*, trans. Jonathan Rosenbaum (New York: Harper & Row, 1972), 10.

26. Ibid., 10.

27. Richard Combs, "Primal Scream: An Interview With Steven Spielberg," *Sight and Sound* 46, no. 2 (Spring 1977):111–13.

28. William Pechter, "Man Bites Shark (& Other Curiosities)," *Commentary*, November 1975, 68.

29. Combs, "Primal Scream," 113.

30. Bazin, *Orson Welles*, 66–67.

31. Douglas Fowler, "*Alien*, *The Thing* and the Principles of Terror," *Studies in Popular Culture* 4 (Spring 1981):19–20.

32. Coursodon with Sâuvage *American Directors*, 2:343.

33. Royal, "Steven Spielberg," 23–24.

34. Mik Cribben, "On Location with *Jaws*," *American Cinematographer* 56, no. 3 (March 1975):276.

35. Ibid., 276.

36. Charles Derry, *Dark Dreams: A Psychological History of the Modern Horror Film* (Cranbury, N.J.: A. S. Barnes & Co., 1977), 81.

37. Gottlieb, *Jaws Log*, 120.

38. Ibid., 118.

39. Fox, *20/20* Interview, 24 June 1982.

40. Royal, "Steven Spielberg," 22.

41. Coursodon with Sâuvage, *American Directors*, 2:343.

42. Fowler, "Principles of Terror," 19.

43. Edith Blake, *The Making of the Movie "Jaws"* (New York, 1975), 63.

44. Marcia Magill, *"Jaws," Films In Review* 26, no. 7 (August–September 1975):436.

45. Derry, *Dark Dreams*, 82.

46. Gottlieb, *Jaws Log*, 206. According to Pye and Myles, *Movie Brats*, 236 this scene is Milius's work. It does bear the hallmarks of his work.

47. Hugh Downs, "20/20" Interview, ABC-TV, 16 June 1983.

48. We are indebted to Steve Hanks for pointing out the subliminal ghosting technique in *Jaws*, which he discovered while teaching Spielberg's techniques to his film class. Hanks, an independent filmmaker, teaches film production at the University of New Orleans.

49. Bazin, *Orson Welles*, 33.

Chapter 4

1. When Spielberg was sixteen, he produced an amateur film entitled *Firelight*, which featured hostile aliens invading earth. An ambitious effort for a young person, it reveals the interest in outer space and extraterrestrials that became more fully developed in *Close Encounters* and *E.T.: The Extra-Terrestrial*. In the course of this development, Spielberg changed his original scenario of "hostile aliens" in *Firelight* to that of "benevolent aliens" coming from the heavens to greet and communicate with earthlings.

2. Pye and Myles, *Movie Brats*, 238; see also Pollock, *Skywalking* 135–36. Part of Lucas's problem in selling *Star Wars* was the script, which some viewed as "incomprehensible." In addition, there was speculation that the special effects could not be achieved.

3. Pye and Myles, *Movie Brats*, 240.

4. Crawley, *Steven Spielberg Story*, 57–62.

5. Ibid., 57–58.

6. Ibid., 59–60.

7. Steven C. Early, *An Introduction to American Movies* (New York: New American Library, 1978), 189; for an extensive discussion of the special effects (created by visual effects supervisor Douglas Trumbull and others), see Douglas Trumbull, "Creating the Photographic Special Effects for *Close Encounters of the Third Kind*" *American Cinematographer* 59, no. 1 (January 1978):74–83, 96–97. See also articles by Spielberg, Herb A. Lightman, Vilmos Zsigmond (director of photography), Joe Alves (production designer), Frank Warner (su-

pervising sound effects editor), and Julia Phillips (producer), in the same issue of *American Cinematographer.*

8. Bob Balaban, *"Close Encounters of the Third Kind" Diary* (New York, 1978), iii.

9. Pye and Myles, *Movie Brats,* 238–41.

10. Ibid., 241.

11. Balaban, *Close Encounters,* 41.

12. "Behind the Scenes of 'Close Encounters of the Third Kind,'" *American Cinematographer* 59, no. 1 (January 1978):26.

13. The structural analysis is based upon *Close Encounters of the Third Kind: Special Edition,* except where noted.

14. This scene was filmed long after the initial photography was completed. Spielberg felt that Truffaut, Laughlin, and the international scene needed to be introduced at the beginning of the film.

15. Jack Kroll, *"Close Encounters of the Third Kind*: The UFO's Are Coming," *Newsweek,* 21 November 1977, 92.

16. Early, *Introduction,* 189.

17. Royal, "Steven Spielberg," 23.

18. Balaban, *Close Encounters,* 39.

19. Raymond M. Olderman, "American Fiction 1974–1976: The People Who Fell to Earth," *Contemporary Literature* 19 no. 4 (1978): 513.

20. The sky effects were created by a young filmmaker named Scott Squires, who had just joined Future General to help with research and development projects; Squires created the unusual cloud formations using a special mixture of white poster paints whipped up in an electric blender. See Douglas Trumbull, "Photographic Effects," 81–82.

21. Kroll, *"Close Encounters,"* 89.

22. Frank Rich, "The Aliens are Coming!" *Time,* 7 November 1977, 104.

23. Kroll, *"Close Encounters,"* 91.

24. Pye and Myles, *Movie Brats,* 244.

25. George Lucas appears to have avoided "message films" altogether since his *THX 1138,* but interestingly, he was set to direct *Apocalypse Now* (originally written by John Milius) in the early seventies under Coppola's Zoetrope Studio.

26. Pye and Myles, *Movie Brats,* 242.

27. Annette Insdorf, *Truffaut* (Boston: Twayne, 1978), 183.

28. Rich, "Aliens," 102.

29. Balaban, *Close Encounters,* 104–106.

30. Carlo Rambaldi, the creator of Spielberg's alien, produced a four-foot-high latex figure that was connected to a series of me-

chanical levers several feet away. Spielberg was so concerned with security that he surrounded the set with guards. According to Balaban, *Close Encounters,* 165, Spielberg did not want to get scooped as he did on *Jaws* when a curious photographer got a picture of the mechanical shark when the tarpin was removed (see Carl Gottlieb, *Jaws Log,* 110). Spielberg and Rambaldi demonstrated the creature to Balaban and Truffaut, pressing levers to make it smile, blink its eyes, and lift its hand. It even had an Adam's apple that moved. Balaban reported that his initial feeling, after seeing Rambaldi's creation, was "miraculous" (168).

31. Balaban, *Close Encounters,* 175.
32. Pye and Myles, *Movie Brats,* 244.
33. Balaban, *Close Encounters,* 174–175.
34. Ibid., 175.
35. Crawley, *Steven Spielberg Story,* 84.
36. Ibid., 85.
37. McCarthy, "Sand Castles," 55.
38. Crawley, *Steven Spielberg Story,* 87.
39. Ibid., 86.
40. Ibid., 86.
41. Pye and Myles, *Movie Brats,* 244.
42. Crawley, *Steven Spielberg Story,* 87.
43. Ibid., 87.
44. Pye and Myles, *Movie Brats,* 241–42.
45. Balaban, *Close Encounters,* 109.
46. Pauline Kael, "Greening," 349.

Chapter 5

1. Coursodon with Sâuvage, *American Directors,* 2:343.
2. According to Chris Hodenfield, "*1941:* Bombs Away!" *Rolling Stone,* 24 January 1980, an interview with Spielberg, both Zemeckis and Gale were students in a USC class (around 1976) taught by screenwriter and director John Milius (a colleague and friend of Spielberg) who encouraged them to develop their original screenplay; Milius reportedly gave the Zemeckis/Gale screenplay the title "The Night the Japs Attacked" when he began showing the script to studios hoping to secure its proposed $6 million budget (37). In addition, the interview notes that when Milius decided to make his surfing movie, *Big Wednesday* (1978) he gave the script to Spielberg (37). According to Crawley, *Steven Spielberg Story,* 77, Zemeckis and Gale wrote the script for John Milius in 1976, and Spielberg was reported to have said, "Gee, John, if you ever get tired and want to

do something else, I'd love to do it." Crawley also confirms that Milius gave the project to Spielberg when he decided to make *Big Wednesday* (77). Crawley, however, never mentions Milius's title, "The Night the Japs Attacked," and refers to the Zemeckis/Gale working titles as either "Hollywood '41" or "The Rising Sun." Bob Balaban, *Close Encounters*, 107, never mentions the title for the screenplay, but describes it as "a Japanese attack on L.A." The general sequence of events that involve Spielberg with Zemeckis, Gale, and *1941* are further confirmed by Spielberg, "Directing *1941*," *American Cinematographer*, 1213.

3. Crawley, *Steven Spielberg Story*, 77.

4. Hodenfield, "*1941*: Bombs Away!" 37.

5. Balaban, *Close Encounters*, 107.

6. As quoted in "Animal House Goes to War," *Time*, 16 April 1979, 97.

7. Spielberg, "Directing *1941*," 1213.

8. Ibid., 1275

9. David S. Reiss, "*1941*: A Conversation with DP William A. Fraker, ASC," *Filmmakers Monthly* 13, no. 2 (December 1979):35.

10. Ibid., 35.

11. Ibid., 35.

12. Ibid., 35.

13. Spielberg, "Directing *1941*," 1251.

14. Ibid., 1258.

15. Ibid., 1258.

16. Ibid., 1258.

17. Crawley, *Steven Spielberg Story*, 79.

18. Reiss, "Conversation," 34.

19. Gerald Mast, *The Comic Mind*, 2d ed. (Chicago and London: The University of Chicago Press, 1979), 26–27.

20. Crawley, *Steven Spielberg Story*, 77.

21. Hodenfield, "*1941*: Bombs Away!" 38.

22. Mast, *Comic Mind*, 4; Mast poses the question whether John Ford is a comic director. In his answer, he decides that Ford is not, that he uses comic touches and characters in films, but the overall aim (in most of his major films) is not comic (4). (Mast clarifies this statement with a footnote, excluding Ford's 1952 film, *The Quiet Man*, adding "By major films I mean the literary adaptations of 1935–41 and the Westerns."). The parallel is therefore drawn to Spielberg, who has been compared to Ford on numerous occasions, and is himself, likewise, not a comic director.

23. Crawley, *Steven Spielberg Story*, 77.

24. Spielberg, "Directing *1941*," 1213.

25. Ibid., 1213.
26. Mast, *Comic Mind*, 26.
27. Ibid., 26.
28. Crawley, *Steven Spielberg Story*, 77.
29. Hodenfield, "*1941:* Bombs Away!" 38.
30. Mast, "Comic Plots" in *Comic Mind*, 4–9; Because Mast's remaining three comic plot devices focus on a central character, they were not applicable to *1941* since the film has no central character. The remaining three comic plots Mast describes are (1) unification by a central figure of the film's action (examples include Don Quixote, Huck Finn, and Augie March); (2) noncomic ends (where a character does a specific task in order to get the girl and pot of gold at the end of the rainbow), and (3) where a central character discovers an error he has made in the course of his life and attempts to correct it.
31. Hodenfield, "*1941:* Bombs Away!" 38.
32. Ibid., 38.
33. Ibid.
34. Ibid.
35. Ibid., 39.
36. Ibid., 38.
37. Crawley, *Steven Spielberg Story*, 79.

Chapter 6

1. "Revising the Rating System," *Newsweek*, 2 July 1984, 45.
2. Pollock, *Skywalking*, 185, 206, 222–30; George Lucas envisioned a serialesque film in which the protagonist, a world-ranging archaeologist named Indiana Smith (Lucas's original name for the character, 224), would find himself in a series of cliff-hanging incidents. While struggling with the script for *Star Wars*, Lucas met with filmmaker Phil Kaufman who suggested interspersing Indiana's adventures with the Lost Ark of the Covenant, described in the book, *Spear of Destiny*, which detailed Adolf Hitler's interest in religious artifacts (222). Over the next three weeks, Lucas and Kaufman exchanged story ideas, but when Kaufman was offered another picture to direct, he dropped the project. Lucas returned to his problematic *Star Wars* script and the idea for *Raiders* went back on the shelf. Spielberg was intrigued by Lucas's idea of a 1930s serial type movie with a playboy adventurer who rescues women and solves mysteries; they promised to make the picture together (185). Spielberg sent Lucas a copy of Lawrence Kasdan's script, *Continental Divide*, late in 1977 to show him Kasdan's crisp writing style which he thought

essential for *Raiders* (206–207). Lucas agreed. By mid-1978, Kasdan had finished the screenplay for *Raiders* and presented it to Lucas (207).

3. Pollock, *Skywalking*, 223.

4. Ibid., 224.

5. Richard Combs, "Primal Scream: An Interview With Steven Spielberg," *Sight and Sound* 46, no. 2 (Spring 1977):113.

6. Spielberg was fascinated with Ridley Scott's *Alien* (1979) which featured an unusual style of diffusion by combining a smoke-filled set with strong backlighting, thus achieving what some critics called a futuristic, *film noir* ambiance. This gave Spielberg the idea to film *Raiders* as a Brechtian *film noir* (see Steven Spielberg, "Of Narrow Misses and Close Calls," *American Cinematographer* 62, no. 11 [November 1981]:1141), although he finally decided to go with Lucas's straightforward approach (see Pollock, *Skywalking*, 223).

7. *The Making of "Raiders of the Lost Ark,"* a behind-the-scenes film produced by George Lucas and Lucasfilm, 1981.

8. Crawley, *Steven Spielberg Story*, 92.

9. Royal, "Steven Spielberg," 21.

10. Jonathan Rosenbaum, "Declarations of Independents: Movies for Chameleons," *Soho News*, 10 June 1981, p.39, cols. 1–4.

11. Crawley, *Steven Spielberg Story*, 96.

12. Pollock, *Skywalking*, 225.

13. Crawley notes, *Steven Spielberg Story*, 29, that "bits of old movies turned up in *Raiders of the Lost Ark*." "Indy's DC-3 flying through the Himalayas to Marion's bar had carried most of the 1973 cast to their *Lost Horizon* and a 30s' street scene came from *The Hindenburg* (1975)" (97). According to Richard Edlund, photographic effects supervisor (Richard Edlund, "Creating the Visual Special Effects for *Raiders*," *American Cinematographer*, 62, no. 11 [November 1981]:1106–08, 1144–51), the flight of the Pan American "China Clipper" sequence was actually a miniature (1108, caption). The scene where Indy and Marion climb aboard the plane was real. In his account Edlund reveals, "We discovered, fortunately, that only about five miles away from I.L.M. [Lucas's Industrial Light and Magic special effects firm] there was a flying boat of the required type in drydock. . . . The actual full-sized flying boat was not in the water. It was on dry land and could not float (1149). From Edlund's detailed account it is unlikely that airplane footage from *Lost Horizon* was used. The use of footage from the film *The Hindenburg* could not be confirmed.

14. Steven Spielberg, "Narrow Misses," 1163.

15. Barbara L. Baker, "It's a Boy's Life: A Rhetorical Examina-

tion of Female Roles in *Raiders of the Lost Ark* and *Conan the Barbarian*" (unpublished paper presented at the University Film and Video Association, Denton, Texas, 4 August 1983), 12.

16. Baker goes on to say that though Marion "can be spunky" in a sort of backhanded tribute to women's liberation, this compliment is edged with insult. Indeed, the eventual message might be interpreted as more of a *backlash* against the women's movement, since it suggests that the price of female self-assertion is to be victimized. In a world where men are either protectors or rapists, it does not do to alienate the protectors. As translated by *Raiders*, this means that Indiana must be portrayed as superior to both Marion and the villains. Furthermore, Marion is punished in various ways for her "uppity" behavior (13).

17. Crawley, *Steven Spielberg Story*, 93.

18. Spielberg, "Narrow Misses," 1164–65.

19. Taylor, *Making of "Raiders,"* picture insert section (see caption).

20. Crawley, *Steven Spielberg Story*, 152.

21. Pollock, *Skywalking*, 223.

22. Royal, "Steven Spielberg," 25.

23. Harper, "Spielberg," 50.

24. Ibid., 50.

25. Jack Kroll, "Indy Strikes Again," *Newsweek*, 4 June 1984, 78.

26. Harper, "Spielberg," 50.

27. Kroll, "Indy Strikes Again," 79.

28. Ibid., 78.

29. Pollock, *Skywalking*, 224.

30. Nancy Griffin, "Jungle Chums: Indy and Willie in a Race with Doom," *Life*, June 1984, 92.

31. Kroll, "Indy Strikes Again," 78.

32. "An Interview with Steven Spielberg," in *Indiana Jones and the Temple of Doom: Official Collectors Edition*, ed. Freeman (New York, 1984), 56.

33. Susan Freeman, "The Most Expensive Train Set in the World," in *Indiana Jones*, 46.

34. Ralph Novak, "*Indiana Jones and the Temple of Doom*," *People*, 4 June 1984, 12.

35. George F. Will, "*Indiana Jones* Oversteps Limits," [*Jackson, Mississippi*] *Clarion-Ledger*, 31 May 1984, p. 15A, cols. 3–4.

36. Kroll, "Indy Strikes Again," 79.

37. Ibid., 79.

38. Harper, "Spielberg," 50.

39. Will, "*Indiana Jones*," p. 15A, cols. 3–4.

Chapter 7

1. Paul M. Sammon, "Turn on Your Heartlight: Inside E.T.," *Cinefex*, no. 11 (January 1983):5.

2. Jack Kroll, "Close Encounter," 98.

3. Sammon, "Heartlight," 10, 13.

4. Crawley, *Steven Spielberg Story*, 136.

5. Sammon, "Heartlight," 13.

6. Marcia Magill, *"Jaws,"* 436, notes that the "programmed shark" was realistic enough for most of its scenes, but "has one truly phony close-up, wearing (as my companion remarked) 'too much make-up.'" Pye and Myles, *Movie Brats*, 244, describe Puck, the "adult E.T." in *Close Encounters of the Third Kind*, as "an image of great grace and beauty and wonder." Other critics, however, appeared dissatisfied with the alien's appearance.

7. Ralph Kaminsky, "Spielberg Discloses Sequel Script at 'Encounters' Press Conference," *Boxoffice*, 21 November 1977, 6.

8. Crawley, *Steven Spielberg Story*, 84.

9. Ibid., 85.

10. Ibid.

11. Ibid.

12. Ibid.

13. Ibid., 107.

14. Ibid., 108.

15. Ibid.

16. Ibid., 141–43. Crawley devotes an entire section, "Let's Talk About Women," to the women who were so important to the film's production.

17. Charles Michener and Katrine Ames, "A Summer Double Punch," *Newsweek*, 31 May 1982, 62.

18. Ibid., 64.

19. Royal, "Steven Spielberg," 19.

20. Ibid., 19.

21. Richard Corliss, "Steve's Summer Magic," *Time*, 31 May 1982, 54.

22. Ibid., 55.

23. Michener and Ames, "Double Punch," 64.

24. Corliss, "Magic," 56.

25. Ibid., 57.

26. Royal "Steven Spielberg," 18.

27. Crawley, *Steven Spielberg Story*, 120.

28. Ibid., 120.

29. Michener and Ames, "Double Punch," 63.

30. Corliss, "Magic," 54–55.

31. Michael Sragow, "Conversation," 26.

32. Ibid., 26.

33. Crawley, *Steven Spielberg Story*, 117.

34. Sragow, "Conversation," 26.

35. Tom O'Brien, "Steven Spielberg's Suburban Animism: Very High Sci-Fi," *Commonweal*, 13 August 1982, 442–43.

36. Sragow, "Conversation," 26.

37. William Kotzwinkle, *E.T.: The Extra-Terrestrial in His Adventures on Earth* (New York, 1982), 231.

38. Ibid., 229.

39. Andrew Epstein, 'The Woman behind the Boom: Melissa Mathison Pens the Bonanza Called 'E.T.,'" *Chicago Tribune*, 15 August 1982, as quoted in Robert Short, *The Gospel from Outer Space* (San Francisco: Harper & Row, 1983), 65.

40. Ibid., 65.

41. Al Millar, *"E.T."—You're More Than a Movie Star* (Newport News, Va: privately published, 1982), 4–5. Millar, a professor of English and biblical literature at Christopher Newport College, Newport News, Virginia, has also written an unpublished humorous account of Universal Studios' reaction to his pamphlet and his subsequent fame, entitled, "The Flea's Reprieve: The Professor Who Saw Jesus in 'E.T.'"

42. Short, *Gospel*, 24.

43. O'Brien, "Animism," 443.

44. Ibid.

45. Ibid., 444.

46. Ibid., 445.

Chapter 8

1. From introductions to the original "Twilight Zone" television series by the show's creator and host, Rod Serling.

2. Crawley, *Steven Spielberg*, 146.

3. David Ansen, "Twilight's Last Gleaming," *Newsweek*, 27 June 1983, 80.

4. Robert Bloch, *Twilight Zone: The Movie* (New York, 1983), 199–200.

5. Ibid., 203.

6. Ansen, "Twilight," 80.

7. Ibid.

8. Ibid.

9. Crawley, *Steven Spielberg Story*, 146.

10. Ibid., 146.

11. Ibid., 146.

12. Ansen, "Twilight," 80; a footnote at the bottom of Ansen's review notes, "Landis and four associates were indicted by a grand jury late last week [third week in June 1983] on charges of involuntary manslaughter" (80).

13. Ibid.

14. Harper, "Spielberg," 54.

Chapter 9

1. Crawley, *Steven Spielberg Story*, 154.

2. Ibid., 17.

3. Spielberg's association with Robert Zemeckis and Bob Gale was apparently the result of his association with John Milius, a friend and colleague of Spielberg as early as 1975 (see Crawley, 75). Hodenfield, "1941: Bombs Away!" 37, specifies that Zemeckis and Gale took a class from John Milius at USC where they developed the *1941* screenplay at Milius's urging. (See note 2, Chapter 5.)

4. Crawley, *Steven Spielberg Story*, 75.

5. Ibid.

6. Ibid.

7. Ibid.

8. Ibid., 76.

9. Ibid., 89.

10. McCarthy, "Sand Castles," 58.

11. Ibid.

12. Sragow, "Conversation," 28.

13. Ibid.

14. Crawley, *Steven Spielberg Story*, 124, 26.

15. Ibid., 127.

16. Corliss, "Magic," 57.

17. Crawley, *Steven Spielberg Story*, 128–29.

18. David Ansen, "Little Toyshop of Horrors," *Newsweek*, 18 June 1984, 90.

19. Ibid.

20. Ibid.

21. Ibid.

22. Ibid.

23. Ibid., 90, 92.

24. Richard Corliss, "I Dream for a Living," *Time*, 15 July 1985, 54–61.

25. Ibid., 55.

26. Leonard Maltin, review of *The Goonies,* "Entertainment To-night," 20 June 1985.

27. Jack Kroll, "Teeny-Boppers' Treasure Hunt," *Newsweek,* 10 June 1985, 88.

28. Ibid.

29. Richard Corliss, "This Way to the Children's Crusade," *Time,* 1 July 1985, 62.

30. Benjamin Morrison, "Li'l Stevie Wunderkind and His 'Amaz-ing' Anthology Series," *Times-Picayune,* 23 June 1985, TV Focus insert, 4, cols. 1–3.

31. Corliss, "I Dream," 61.

32. *"The Color Purple," Daily Variety,* 16 December 1985, p. 3, col. 1; p. 13, col. 4.

33. Richard Corliss, "The Three Faces of Steve," *Time,* 23 December 1985, 78.

34. Alice Walker, *The Color Purple* (New York: Harcourt Brace Jovanovich, 1982), 176.

35. Thadious M. Davis, "Alice Walker's Celebration of Self in Southern Generations," in *Women Writers of the Contemporary South,* ed. Peggy Whitman Prenshaw (Jackson, Miss.: University Press of Mississippi, 1984), 51–52.

Selected Bibliography

Novelizations and Memorabilia

Bloch, Robert. *Twilight Zone: The Movie.* New York: Warner Books, 1983. A novelization by Bob Bloch of all four segments from the respective screenplays.

Freeman, Susan, ed. *Indiana Jones and the Temple of Doom: Official Collectors Edition.* New York: Paradise Press, 1984. A publication that is extensively illustrated with stills from the film. It gives a brief synopsis of the story and describes many of the special effects used in the film, most notably the construction of the miniature mining car railway system, which was photographed with a modified Nikon 35-mm still camera in the VistaVision format.

Gripe, George. *Gremlins.* New York: Avon Books, 1984. A novelization of Chris Columbus's screenplay.

Kahn, James. *Indiana Jones and the Temple of Doom.* New York: Ballantine Books, 1984. A novelization of George Lucas's story from Gloria Katz and Willard Huyck's screenplay.

Kotzwinkle, William. *E.T.: The Extra-Terrestrial in His Adventures on Earth.* New York: Berkley Books, 1982. A novelization of Melissa Mathison's screenplay based on Steven Spielberg's original story. It is interesting to note that in Kotzwinkle's novelization, the story begins from the point of view of Elliott's mother, but eventually shifts to Elliott; in the film, the action is always from Elliott's point of view.

Letters to E.T. Introduction by Steven Spielberg. New York: G.P. Putnam's Sons, 1983. A book containing letters written to Spielberg from both children and adults after seeing *E.T.: The Extra-Terrestrial.*

Spielberg, Steven. *Close Encounters of the Third Kind.* New York: Dell Publishing Co., 1977. A novelization of Steven Spielberg's original screenplay. Although Spielberg is credited with the novelization, it was most probably written by a ghostwriter.

Books On Spielberg and His Work

Balaban, Bob. *"Close Encounters of the Third Kind" Diary.* New York: Paradise Press, 1977. A behind-the-scenes account of filming

170

Close Encounters; the book includes many interesting and funny episodes that occurred on location.

Blake, Edith. *The Making of the Movie "Jaws".* New York: Ballantine Books, 1975.

Cagin, Seth and Philip Dray. *Hollywood Films of the Seventies: Sex, Drugs, Violence, Rock 'n' Roll and Politics.* New York: Harper & Row, 1984.

Coursodon, Jean-Pierre, with Pierre Sâuvage. American Directors. Vol. 2. New York: McGraw-Hill Book Co. 1983.

Crawley, Tony. *The Steven Spielberg Story: The Man behind the Movies.* New York: Quill Press, 1983. Compiled mostly from news accounts and press releases, Crawley traces Spielberg from his youth to the making of *E.T.* The book is filled with typos and the British colloquialisms are sometimes difficult to understand. The book also contains several inaccuracies.

Gerani, Gary with Paul H. Schulman. *Fantastic Televison.* New York: Harmony Books, 1977.

Gottlieb, Carl. *The Jaws Log.* New York: Dell Publishing Co., 1975. A rigorous account of the difficulties encountered during the filming of *Jaws*; illustrated.

Millar, Al. *"E.T."—You're More Than a Movie Star.* Newport News, Va.: privately published, 1982. This short pamphlet contains the thirty-three parallels to the Christ story Millar originally noticed. Since it was published, Millar has found additional parallels and plans to publish them, as well as a humorous account of his tangle with Universal Studios, in another work entitled, "The Flea's Reprieve: The Professor Who Saw Jesus in 'E.T.'"

Pollock, Dale. *Skywalking: The Life and Films of George Lucas.* New York: Harmony Books, 1983. An extensive biography of the life and times of George Lucas. Of major interest are Lucas's association with Francis Ford Coppola and Zoetrope Studios, his disagreements with the studio over *THX 1138* and *American Grafitti*, the evolution of the *Star Wars* saga, his retreat from directing, and his association with Steven Spielberg.

Pye, Michael, and Linda Myles. *The Movie Brats.* New York: Holt, Rinehart and Winston, 1979. A good overview of contemporary directors (aptly dubbed "the movie brats") and their films. The book features such directors as Francis Ford Coppola, Martin Scorsese, Brian De Palma, John Milius, and others. The first part of the book lays the foundation for its unusual title.

Taylor, Derek. *The Making of "Raiders of the Lost Ark."* New York: Ballantine Books, 1981.

Biographical Articles

Ames, Katrine. "E.T.'s Best Friend." *Newsweek*, 21 June 1982, p. 65. An article on the life of child actor Henry Thomas, who played Elliott in *E.T.*

"Animal House Goes to War." *Time*, 16 April 1979, p. 97.

Ansen, David. "Little Toyshop of Horrors." *Newsweek*, 18 June 1984, p. 90, 92. A review of *Gremlins*.

————. "Twilight's Last Gleaming." *Newsweek*, 27 June 1983, p. 80. A review of *Twilight Zone: The Movie*.

Breskin, David. "Steven Spielberg." *Rolling Stone*, 24 October 1985, pp. 22–24, 70–80. Spielberg discusses "Amazing Stories," *The Color Purple*, his son, Max, and his future projects.

Callo, Jim. "Director Steven Spielberg Takes the Wraps off E.T., Revealing His Secrets at Last." *People*, 23 August 1982, pp. 80–88.

"*Close Encounters of the Third Kind*," *American Cinematographer* 59, no. 1 (January 1978), special issue. This issue is almost entirely dedicated to the film, *Close Encounters*, with articles by Steven Spielberg and special effects wizard Douglas Trumbull.

"*The Color Purple*." *Daily Variety*, 16 December 1985, p. 3, col. 1; p. 13, col. 4. A review of *The Color Purple*.

Combs, Richard. "Primal Scream: An Interview with Steven Spielberg." *Sight and Sound* 46, no. 2 (Spring 1977):111–13.

Cooper, Arthur. "The Naked Tooth." *Newsweek*, 23 June 1975, p. 54. A review of *Jaws*.

Corliss, Richard. "I Dream for a Living." *Time*, 15 July 1985, pp. 54–61. A retrospective look at Spielberg's career occasioned by the rerelease of his 1982 fantasy-adventure film, *E.T.: The Extra-Terrestrial*.

————. "Steve's Summer Magic." *Time*, 31 May 1982, pp. 54–60. A review of *E.T.: The Extra-Terrestrial* and *Poltergeist*.

————. "This Way to the Children's Crusade." *Time*, 1 July 1985, p. 62. A review of *The Goonies* and *Back to the Future*.

————. "Three Faces of Steve." *Time*, 23 December 1985, p. 78. A review of *The Color Purple*.

Cribben, Mik. "On Location with *Jaws*." *American Cinematographer* 56, no. 3 (March 1975):274–77, 320, 330–31, 350–51.

"*E.T.: The Extra-Terrestrial*." *American Cinematographer* 64, no. 1 (January 1983):46–54. Special feature: articles by George E. Turner, Allen D. Lowell, and Lloyd Kent.

"The Filming of *1941*." *American Cinematographer* 60, no. 12 (December 1979):1206–29. Special feature: articles by Steven Spielberg, Gregory Jein, A. D. Flowers, Deborah K. Melton, David W. Samuelson.

Griffin, Nancy. "Jungle Chums: Indy and Willie in a Race with Doom." *Life*, June 1984, pp.88–94.

Harper, Suzanne. "Spielberg." *Nutshell: The Magazine for the College Community*. Spring 1984, pp. 49–54. Harper's interview gives a good overview of Spielberg's recollections directing *Temple of Doom*. The interview concludes with several of Spielberg's upcoming projects as of 1984.

Hodenfield, Chris. "*1941*: Bombs Away!" *Rolling Stone*, 24 January 1980, pp. 37–39, 41–42. The article discusses many of the film's problems and why it does not work as a comedy. Spielberg is also interviewed; he discusses the making of the film and the problems encountered during production.

Kaminski, Ralph. "Spielberg Discloses Sequel Script at *Encounters* Press Conference." *Boxoffice*, 21 November 1977, p. 6. An interesting press blurb considering Spielberg did not come up with the "Night Skies" project until 1978.

Kroll, Jack. "Close Encounter with Steven Spielberg." *Newsweek*, 21 November 1977, pp. 98–99.

———. "*Close Encounters of the Third Kind*: The UFO's Are Coming." *Newsweek*, 21 November 1977, pp. 88–89, 91–97.

———. "Indy Strikes Again." *Newsweek*, 4 June 1984, pp. 78–79.

———. "Teeny-Boppers' Treasure Hunt." *Newsweek*, 10 June 1985, p. 88. A review of *The Goonies*.

McCarthy, Todd. "Sand Castles." *Film Comment* 18, no. 3 (May–June 1982):53–59. A retrospective of Spielberg's career up to *E.T.*

Magill, Marsha. "Film Reviews: *Jaws*." *Films in Review* 26, no. 7 (August–September 1975):436.

Mandell, Paul. "*Poltergeist*: Stilling the Restless Animus." *Cinefex*, no. 10 (October 1982):4–39. *Cinefex* is one of the best and most thorough magazines dedicated to behind-the-scenes special effects. The magazine is superbly printed with detailed illustrations and pictures.

Marill, Alvin H. "Film Reviews: *Sugarland Express*." *Films in Review* 25, no. 5 (May 1974):307–8.

Michener, Charles and Katrine Ames. "A Summer Double Punch." *Newsweek*, 31 May 1982, pp. 62–64. Reviews of *E.T.: The Extra-Terrestrial* and *Poltergeist*.

Morrison, Benjamin. "Li'l Stevie Wunderkind and His 'Amazing' Anthology Series." *Times-Picayune*, 23 June 1985, TV Focus insert, p. 4, cols. 1–3.

Novack, Ralph. "*Indiana Jones and the Temple of Doom*." *People*, 4 June 1984, p. 12.

O'Brien, Tom. "Steven Spielberg's Suburban Animism: Very High

Sci-Fi." *Commonweal*, 13 August 1982, pp. 442–45. A commentary on Spielberg's films *Close Encounters of the Third Kind* and *E.T.: The Extra-Terrestrial* and the director's interest in UFOs.

"*Raiders of the Lost Ark* and How It Was Filmed." *American Cinematographer* 62, no. 11 (November 1981):1096–1110. Special feature: articles by Steven Spielberg, cinematographer Douglas Slocombe, and special effects wizard Richard Edlund.

Rich, Frank. "The Aliens are Coming." *Time*, 7 November 1977, pp.102–104. A review of *Close Encounters of the Third Kind*.

Reiss, David. "*1941*: A Conversation with DP William A. Fraker, ASC." *Filmmakers Monthly* 13, no. 2 (December 1979):34–39. A technical view of the photographic techniques used by William Fraker in filming *1941*. Of interest is the use of fog while filming the miniatures.

———. "*Raiders of the Lost Ark*: An Interview with Steven Spielberg." *Filmmakers Monthly* 14, no. 9/10 (July–August 1981):30–39.

Royal, Susan. "Steven Spielberg in His Adventures on Earth." *American Premiere*, 10 July 1982, pp.17–25. An in-depth interview with Steven Spielberg describing himself, his career, his previous films, and his ultimate achievement, *E.T.: The Extra-Terrestrial*.

Sammon, Paul M. "Turn On Your Heartlight: Inside E.T." *Cinefex*, no. 11 (January 1983):4–49. An excellent behind-the-scenes look at the special effects for *E.T.: The Extra-Terrestrial*. Beautifully illustrated with detailed artwork and full-color photographs.

Spielberg, Steven. "Directing 1941." American Cinematographer 60, no. 12 (December 1979):1212–15, 1251, 1258–59, 1275–76. This issue includes articles by others who worked on the film. It also includes a section on the special effects photography and on filming the miniature sets. The extensive use of the Louma crane (a new, highly versatile camera crane) is described in many of the articles.

Sragow, Michael. "A Conversation with Steven Spielberg." *Rolling Stone*, 22 July 1982, pp. 24–26, 28. It is in this article that Spielberg reveals he has matured as a film director and that he has an entirely new perspective on himself and the films he will produce and direct in the future.

"Summer of the Shark." *Time*, 23 June 1975, pp. 42–44, 49–50. A review of *Jaws*.

Tuchman, Mitch. "Close Encounter with Steven Spielberg." *Film Comment*, 14, no. 1 (January–February 1978):49–55. An interview with Steven Spielberg.

Will, George F. "*Indiana Jones* Oversteps Limits." [*Jackson, Miss.*] *Clarion-Ledger*, 31 May 1984, p.15A, cols. 3–4.

Worrell, Denise. "The Autobiography of Peter Pan." *Time*, 15 July 1985, pp. 62–63. An interview with Steven Spielberg.

Zimmerman, Paul. "Hard Riders." *Newsweek*, 8 April 1974, pp. 82–83. A review of *The Sugarland Express*.

Critical Articles

Arkush, Allan. "I Remember Film School." *Film Comment* 19, no. 6 (November–December 1983):57–59. Arkush writes his personal account as a student going to film school during the sixties at New York University.

Baker, Barbara L. "It's a Boy's Life: A Rhetorical Examination of Female Roles in *Raiders of the Lost Ark* and *Conan the Barbarian*." Paper presented to the University Film Association, Denton, Texas, August 1983. In both these films, Baker examines the role of the female, which she perceives as largely stereotypical and almost always subservient to male characters.

Fowler, Douglas. "*Alien, The Thing* and the Principles of Terror." *Studies in Popular Culture* 4 (Spring 1981):16–23. Fowler's article is an excellent treatise on the principles of terror; it sights many film examples, including *Jaws*, and draws interesting conclusions about what scares film audiences.

Pechter, William S. "Man Bites Shark (& Other Curiosities)." *Commentary*, November 1975, pp. 68–72. Pechter's article reflects on Spielberg's *Jaws* and other films released during the summer of 1975.

"Revising the Rating System." *Newsweek*, 2 July 1984, p. 45. A brief article on the events which led to the addition of PG-13, a new rating code for motion pictures.

Rosenbaum, Jonathan. "Declarations of Independents: Movies for Chameleons." *Soho News*, 10 June 1981, p.39. Rosenbaum reviews *Raiders of the Lost Ark* and several other summer releases of 1981.

Televised Sources

Cavett, Dick, host. Interview with Steven Spielberg. "DC." Public Broadcasting Company, 1981. The "DC" show was originally produced by WNET-TV, New York, and aired on 2 July 1981.

Cavett, Dick, host. Interview with Steven Spielberg. "DC." Public Broadcasting Company, 1981. This two-part "DC" show was originally produced by WNET-TV, New York, and aired on 17 June 1981.

Downs, Hugh. Interview with John Williams. "20/20." ABC-TV, 16 June 1983.

Fox, Steve. Interview with Steven Spielberg. "20/20." ABC-TV, 24 June 1982.

Hartman, David, host. Interview with Leah Adler. "Good Morning America." ABC-TV, 5 May 1983.

Maltin, Leonard. Review of *The Goonies.* "Entertainment Tonight." WDSU-TV Channel 4, New Orleans, Louisiana, 20 June 1985 (6:30 P.M. CST).

The Making of "Raiders of the Lost Ark." Produced by George Lucas and Lucasfilm, 1981.

Filmography

Made-for-Television Movies

Something Evil (CBS Television, 1970)
Cast: Sandy Dennis, Darren McGavin, Ralph Bellamy, Jeff Corey,
    Johnnie Whitaker, John Rubinstein
Running Time: 73 minutes
Note: This made-for-television movie was considered above
average with excellent performances given by the cast. The plot
concerns the Worden family's purchase of an old house with an evil
presence. This film is noted for its flippant, offbeat pace combined
with the matter-of-fact presentation of horror.

Duel (Universal, 1971)
Screenplay: Richard Matheson
Cast: Dennis Weaver (David Mann), Jacqueline Scott (Mrs. Mann),
    Eddie Firestone (Café Owner), Lou Frizzell (Bus Driver)
Running time: 73 minutes
Note: Originally telecast in 1971, this film put Spielberg on the
map as an up-and-coming television director. The film was
reedited to expand its running time to ninety minutes for
theatrical release.

Savage (Universal, 1973)
Cast: Martin Landau, Barbara Bain, Will Geer, Paul Richards,
    Michelle Carey, Barry Sullivan, Susan Howard, Dabney
    Coleman, Pat Harrington
Running Time: 74 minutes
Note: An average made-for-television movie that was a pilot for a
prospective Landau-Bain series. The plot concerned an
investigative reporter's search into the past of a Supreme Court
nominee.

Feature Films

Duel (Universal, 1973)
Producer: George Eckstein
Assistant Director: Jim Fargo
Screenplay: Richard Matheson
Director of Photography: Jack A. Marta
Art Director: Robert S. Smith
Set Decorator: S. Blydenburgh
Music: Billy Goldenberg
Editor: Frank Morriss
Cast: Dennis Weaver (David Mann), Jacqueline Scott (Mrs. Mann),
    Eddie Firestone (Café Owner), Lou Frizzell (Bus Driver)
Running time: 90 minutes
Color by: Technicolor

The Sugarland Express (Universal, 1974)
Producers: Richard D. Zanuck and David Brown
Production Executive: William S. Gilmore, Jr.
Assistant Director: James Fargo
Screenplay: Steven Spielberg, Hal Barwood and Matthew Robbins
Director of Photography: Vilmos Zsigmond
Production Designer: Joseph Alves, Jr.
Music: John Williams
Additional Music: "Toots" Thielemans (harmonica solos)
Editors: Edward M. Abroms and Verna Fields
Cast: Goldie Hawn (Lou Jean), Ben Johnson (Captain Tanner),
    Michael Sacks (Slide), William Atherton (Clovis), Gregory
    Walcott (Mashburn), Steve Kanaly (Jessup), Louise Latham
    (Mrs. Loony), Harrison Zanuck (Baby Langston), A.L. Camp
    (Mr. Knocker), Jessie Lee Fulton (Mrs. Knocker)
RunningTime: 109 minutes
Color by: Technicolor
Rating: PG

Jaws (Universal, 1975)
Producers: Richard D. Zanuck and David Brown
Assistant Director: Tom Joyner
Screenplay: Peter Benchley and Carl Gottlieb
Director of Photography: Bill Butler
Live Shark Footage: Ron and Valerie Taylor
Production Designer: Joseph Alves, Jr.

Set Decorator: John M. Dwyer
Music: John Williams
Editor: Verna Fields
Special Effects: Robert A. Mattey
Cast: Roy Scheider (Brody), Robert Shaw (Quint), Richard
    Dreyfuss (Hooper), Lorraine Gary (Ellen Brody), Murray
    Hamilton (Mayor Vaughn), Carl Gottlieb (Meadows), Jeffrey
    Kramer (Hendricks), Peter Benchley (TV interviewer)
Running Time: 124 minutes
Color by: Technicolor
Rating: R

Close Encounters Of The Third Kind (Columbia Pictures, 1977)
Producers: Julia Phillips and Michael Phillips
Associate Producer: Clark Paylow
Assistant Director: Chuck Myers
Screenplay: Steven Spielberg
Director of Photography: Vilmos Zsigmond
Director of Photography (Additional American scenes): William A.
    Fraker
Director of Photography (Special sequences, India): Douglas
    Slocombe
Production Designer: Joseph Alves, Jr.
Set Decorator: Phil Abramson
Music: John Williams
Editor: Michael Kahn
Special Effects: Douglas Trumbull
Visual Effects Concepts: Steven Spielberg
Cast: Richard Dreyfuss (Roy Neary), François Truffaut (Claude
    Lacombe), Teri Garr (Ronnie Neary), Melinda Dillon (Jullian
    Guiler), Bob Balaban (David Laughlin), Cary Guffey (Barry
    Guiler), Lance Hendriksen (Robert), Warren Kemmerling (Wild
    Bill)
Running Time: 135 minutes
Rating: PG
Note: For the special edition released in 1980, Spielberg reedited
the film to tighten the midsection and add additional alien-
encounter material and several scenes photographed by Allen
Daviau. The reissue was three minutes shorter than the original
(132 minutes). For the television premiere, Spielberg reedited the
film inserting additional scenes previously filmed but never seen
before. The running time for this version was ten minutes longer
than the original (145 minutes).

1941 (Universal, 1979)
Executive Producer: John Milius
Producer: Buzz Feitshans
Associate Producers: Michael Kahn and Janet Healy
Assistant Directors: Jerry Ziesmer and Steve Perry
Screenplay: Robert Zemeckis and Bob Gale
Story by: Robert Zemeckis, Bob Gale and John Milius
Director of Photography: William A. Fraker
Production Designer: Dean Edward Mitzner
Set Decoration: John Austin
Music: John Williams
Editor: Michael Kahn
Special Effects: A. D. Flowers
Executive in Charge of Production: John Wilson
Cast: Dan Aykroyd (Sergeant Tree), Ned Beatty (Ward Douglas),
    John Belushi (Wild Bill Kelso), Lorraine Gary (Joan Douglas),
    Murray Hamilton (Claude), Christopher Lee (Von
    Kleinschmidt), Tim Matheson (Birkhead), Nancy Allen
    (Donna), Toshiro Mifune (Commander Mitamura), Treat
    Williams (Sitarski), Bobby DiCicco (Wally), Perry Lang
    (Dennis), Dianne Kay (Betty), John Candy (Foley), Eddie
    Deezen (Herbie), Warren Oates (Maddox), Robert Stack
    (General Stilwell), Slim Pickens (Hollis Wood)
Running Time: 120 minutes
Color by: Metrocolor
Rating: PG

Raiders Of The Lost Ark (Paramount Pictures, 1981)
Executive Producers: George Lucas and Howard Kazanjian
Producer: Frank Marshall
Associate Producer: Robert Watts
Assistant Director: David Tomblin
Screenplay: Lawrence Kasdan
Story by: George Lucas and Philip Kaufman
Director of Photography: Douglas Slocombe
Production Designer: Norman Reynolds
Set Decorator: Leslie Dilley
Music: John Williams
Editor: Michael Kahn
Special Visual effects: Industrial Light and Magic
Cast: Harrison Ford (Indiana Jones), Karen Allen (Marion), Paul
    Freeman (Belloq), Ronald Lacey (Toht), John Rhys-Davies
    (Sallah), Denholm Elliot (Brody), Alfred Molina (Satipo), Wolf

Kahler (Dietrich), Anthony Higgins (Gobler), Vic Tablian
(Barranca), Don Fellows (Col. Musgrove), William Hootkins
(Major Eaton)
Running Time: 113 minutes
Rating: G

E.T.: The Extra-Terrestrial (Universal, 1982)
Producers: Steven Spielberg and Kathleen Kennedy
Associate Producer: Melissa Mathison
Assistant Director: Katie Emde
Screenplay: Melissa Mathison
Director of Photography: Allen Daviau
Production Designer: James D. Bissell
Set Decorator: Jackie Carr
Music: John Williams
Editor: Carol Littleton
E.T. Created by: Carlo Rambaldi
Visual Effects Supervisor: Dennis Muren
Special Visual Effects: Industrial Light and Magic
Cast: Henry Thomas (Elliott), Drew Barrymore (Gertie), Robert
MacNaughton (Michael), Dee Wallace (Mary), Peter Coyote
(Keys)
Color by: Deluxe (principal photography) and Technicolor (release
prints)
Running Time: 121 minutes
Rating: G

Twilight Zone: The Movie (Warner Bros., 1983)
Executive Producer: Frank Marshall
Producers; Steven Spielberg and John Landis
Music: Jerry Goldsmith
Segment #1:
Director: John Landis
Screenplay: John Landis
Director of Photography: Stevan Larner
Editor: Malcolm Campbell
Cast: Dan Aykroyd (Passenger), Albert Brooks (Driver), Vic Morrow
(Bill Conner), Doug McGrath (Larry), Charles Hallahan (Ray),
Remus Peets (German officer), Kai Wulff (German officer)
Segment #2 ("Kick the Can"):
Director: Steven Spielberg
Story: George Clayton Johnson

Screenplay: George C. Johnson, Richard Matheson and Josh Rogan
Director of Photography: Allen Daviau
Editor: Michael Kahn
Cast: Scatman Crothers (Mr. Bloom), Bill Quinn (Mr. Conroy),
   Helen Shaw (Mrs. Dempsey), Martin Garner (Mr. Weinstein),
   Christopher Eisenmann (Young Mr. Mute), Laura Mooney
   (Young Mrs. Dempsey), Scott Nemes (Young Mr. Weinstein),
   Tanya Fenmore (Young Mrs. Weinstein), Evan Richards (Young
   Mr. Agee)
Segment #3:
Director: Joe Dante
Screenplay: Richard Matheson
Story by: Jerome Bixby
Director of Photography: John Hora
Editor: Tina Hirsch
Cast: Kathleen Quinlan (Helen Foley), Jeremy Licht (Anthony),
   William Schallert (Anthony's "Father"), Patricia Barry
   (Anthony's "Mother"), Kevin McCarthy (Uncle Walt), Nancy
   Cartwright (Ethel), Dick Miller (Counterman), Billy Mumy
   (Cameo—Boy in Diner)
Segment #4 (remake of "Nightmare at 20,000 Feet"):
Director: George Miller
Story by: Richard Matheson
Screenplay: Richard Matheson
Director of Photography: Allen Daviau
Editor: Howard Smith
Cast: John Lithgow (Mr. Valentine), Abbe Lane (Diana), Donna
   Dixon (Shelly), Charles Knopf (Sky Marshal), John Dennis
   Johnston (Co-pilot), Christina Nigra (Young Passenger), Frank
   Marshall (Ground Engineer), Jeffrey Lampert (Ground
   Engineer)
Running Time: 102 minutes
Rating: PG

Indiana Jones And The Temple Of Doom (Paramount Pictures,
   1984)
Executive Producers: Frank Marshall and George Lucas
Producer: Robert Watts
Associate Producer: Kathleen Kennedy
Story by: George Lucas
Screenplay: Gloria Katz and Willard Huyck
Director of Photography: Douglas Slocombe
Special Visual Effects: Industrial Light and Magic

Music: John Williams
Editor: Michael Kahn
Cast: Harrison Ford (Indy), Kate Capshaw (Willie Scott), Ke Huy
 Quan (Short Round), Amrish Puri (Mola Ram), Roshan Seth
 (Chatter Lal), Phillip Stone (Captain Blumburtt), Roy Chiao
 (Lao Che), David Yip (Wu Han)
Running Time: 118 minutes
Rating: PG

The Color Purple (Warner Bros., 1985)
Executive Producers: Jon Peters and Peter Guber
Producers: Steven Spielberg, Frank Marshall, Kathleen Kennedy,
 and Quincy Jones
Associate Producer: Carol Isenberg
Assistant Directors: Pat Kehoe and Richard Alexander Wells
Screenplay: Menno Meyjes (based on the novel by Alice Walker)
Director of Photography: Allen Daviau
Production Designer: J. Michael Riva
Set Decoration: Linda DeScenna
Art Director: Robert W. Welch
Music: Quincy Jones
Editor: Michael Kahn
Sound: Willie Burton
Casting: Reuben Cannon & Associates
Cast: Danny Glover (Mr./Albert), Whoopi Goldberg (Celie),
 Margaret Avery (Shug Avery), Oprah Winfrey (Sofia), Willard
 Pugh (Harpo), Akosua Busia (Nettie), Desreta Jackson (Young
 Celie), Adolph Caesar (Mr.'s Father), Rae Dawn Chong
 (Squeak), Dana Ivey (Miss Millie)
Running Time: 152 minutes
Color by: DeLuxe
Rating: PG-13

Executive Producer Only

I Wanna Hold Your Hand (Universal, 1978)
Executive Producer: Steven Spielberg
Producer: Tamara Asseyev and Alex Rose
Director: Robert Zemeckis
Screenplay: Robert Gale and Robert Zemeckis
Director of Photography: Donald M. Morgan

Editor: Frank Morriss
Cast: Nancy Allen (Pam Mitchell), Bobby DiCicco (Tony Smerko), Marc McClure (Larry Dubois), Susan Kendall Newman (Janis Goldman), Theresa Saldana (Grace Corrigan), Will Jordan (Ed Sullivan), Eddie Deezen (Richard "Ringo" Klaus)
Running Time: 104 minutes
Rating: PG

Used Cars (Columbia, 1980)
Executive Producer: Steven Spielberg
Producer: Robert Gale
Director: Robert Zemeckis
Screenplay: Robert Gale and Robert Zemeckis
Director of Photography: Donald M. Morgan
Stunts: Terry J. Leonard
Music: Patrick Williams
Editor: Michael Kahn
Cast: Kurt Russell (Rudy Russo), Jack Warden (Roy L. Fuchs and Luke Fuchs), Gerrit Graham (Jeff), Frank McRae (Jim the Mechanic), Deborah Harmon (Barbara Fuchs), Joseph P. Flaherty (Sam Slaton), David L. Lander (Freddie Paris), Michael McKean (Eddie Winslow), Michael Talbott (Mickey)
Running Time: 111 minutes
Rating: R

Poltergeist (Metro-Goldwyn-Mayer, 1982)
Producers: Steven Spielberg and Frank Marshall
Associate Producer: Kathleen Kennedy
Director: Tobe Hooper
Assistant Director: Pat Kehoe
Screenplay: Steven Spielberg, Michael Grais, and Mark Victor
Story by: Steven Spielberg
Director of Photography: Matthew F. Leonetti
Production Designer: James H. Spencer
Set Decorator: Cheryal Kearney
Music: Jerry Goldsmith
Editors: Michael Kahn
Cast: Craig T. Nelson (Steve Freeling), JoBeth Williams (Diane Freeling), Beatrice Straight (Dr. Lesh), Dominique Dunne (Dana Freeling), Oliver Robins (Robbie Freeling), Heather O'Rourke (Carol Anne Freeling), Zelda Rubenstein (Psychic)
Running Time: 111 minutes
Rating: R

Gremlins (Warner Bros., 1984)
Executive Producers: Steven Spielberg, Frank Marshall, and
    Kathleen Kennedy
Producer: Michael Finnell
Director: Joe Dante
Screenplay: Chris Columbus
Director of Photography: John Hora
Production Designer: James H. Spencer
Set Decorator: Jackie Carr
Music: Jerry Goldsmith
Editor: Tina Hirsch
Cast: Zach Galligan (Billy), Phoebe Cates (Kate), Hoyt Axton (Rand
    Peltzer), Polly Holliday (Mrs.Deagle), Frances Lee McCain
    (Lynn Peltzer), Keye Luke (Grandfather), John Louie (Chinese
    Boy), Don Steele (Rockin' Ricky Rialto), Susan Burgess (Little
    Girl), Scott Brady (Sheriff Frank), Corey Feldman (Pete), Arnie
    Moore (Pete's Father)
Running Time: 105 minutes
Rating: PG

The Goonies (Warner Bros., 1985)
Executive Producers: Steven Spielberg, Frank Marshall, and
    Kathleen Kennedy
Producers: Richard Donner and Harvey Bernhard
Director: Richard Donner
Story by: Steven Spielberg
Screenplay: Chris Columbus
Director of Photography: Nick McLean
Production Designer: J. Michael Riva
Art Director: Rick Carter
Set Decorator: Linda DeScenna
Music: Dave Grusin
Editor: Michael Kahn
Cast: Sean Astin (Mikey), Corey Feldman (Mouth), Jeff B. Cohen
    (Chunk), Ke Huy Quan (Data), Josh Brolin (Brand), Kerri
    Green (Andy), Martha Plimpton (Stef), John Matuszak (Sloth),
    Anne Ramsey (Ma Fratelli), Robert Davi (Jake), Joe Pantoliano
    (Francis)
Running Time: 111 minutes
Rating: PG

Back To The Future (Universal, 1985)
Executive Producers: Steven Spielberg, Frank Marshall, and
    Kathleen Kennedy

Producer: Bob Gale and Neil Canton
Director: Robert Zemeckis
Screenplay: Robert Zemeckis and Bob Gale
Director of Photography: Dean Cundey
Music: Alan Silvestri
Editors: Arthur Schmidt and Harry Keramidas
Cast: Michael J. Fox (Marty McFly), Crispin Glover (Mr. McFly) Lea
    Thompson (Mrs. McFly), Christopher Lloyd (Dr. Brown),
    Thomas F. Wilson (Biff), Claudia Wells (Jennifer Parker),
    Wendie Jo Sperber (Linda McFly), George DiCenzo (Sam
    Baines), James Tolkan (the principal, Mr. Strickland)
Running Time: 111 minutes
rating: PG

Young Sherlock Holmes (Paramount Pictures, 1985)
Executive Producers: Steven Spielberg, Frank Marshall, and
    Kathleen Kennedy
Producer: Mark Johnson
Associate Producer: Harry Benn
Director: Barry Levinson
Assistant Director: Michael Murray
Screenplay: Chris Columbus
Director of Photography: Steven Goldblatt, B.S.C.
Special Visual Effects: Industrial Light and Magic
Production Designer: Norman Reynolds
Second Unit Director: Andrew Grieve
Second Unit Director of Photography: Steven Smith
Set Decoration: Michael Ford
Art Directors: Fred Hole and Charles Bishop
Music: Bruce Broughton
Editor: Stu Linder
Cast: Nicholas Rowe (Sherlock Holmes), Alan Cox (John Watson),
    Sophie Ward (Elizabeth), Anthony Higgins (Rathe), Susan
    Fleetwood (Mrs. Dribb), Freddie Jones (Cragwitch), Nigel
    Stock (Waxflatter), Roger Ashton-Griffiths (Lestrade), Earl
    Rhodes (Dudley), Brian Oulton (Master Snelgrove), Patrick
    Newell (Bobster), Donald Eccles (Reverend Nesbitt)
Running Time: 122 minutes
Rating: PG-13

The Money Pit (Universal, 1985)
Note: This film was being readied for a 1985 Christmas release
    when it was shelved at the last minute. In a recent interview,

however, Spielberg mentioned that the film was slated for either a "Christmas release or later in the winter." Spielberg also commented that he was pleased with the film and that it was very funny. It is expected that *The Money Pit* will be released in early 1986 or rescheduled for a summer release date. Directed by Richard Benjamin (*My Favorite Year*), the film stars Tom Hanks and Shelley Long as a young couple who buy an old house on Long Island and discover it needs more work than they thought.

Projects in Progress

(Authors' Note: In recent years, Spielberg's output as an executive producer as well as a writer-director has been phenomenal. In 1985 alone, his company—Amblin Entertainment—turned out no less than five feature films and a season's worth of "Amazing Stories" teleplays, two of which were directed by Spielberg himself. Trying to keep our book up to date prior to publication has almost been impossible. The following is a summary of projects in progress, compiled from the most recent in-depth interview with Steven Spielberg in *Rolling Stone* [24 October 1985]. The reader should bear in mind that Spielberg's many projects in progress change constantly in both order and priority; in addition, because of his concern for security surrounding his projects, Spielberg often disguises them with misleading titles [*E.T.*'s working title was *A Boy's Life*] and often offers misleading information to inquiring reporters and interviewers.)

Spielberg's plans for a remake of *A Guy Named Joe*, to have been called *Always*, was pushed back for another year or two (as was his version of *Peter Pan*) because of *The Color Purple*. Plans are still progressing for *Always*, but Spielberg mentioned he will rename the film because of another film recently released with that title.

Peter Pan, in the planning stages for several years now, seems to be the next feature film project he will direct in 1986. At one time it was rumored that rock star Michael Jackson (who appeared in Sidney Lumet's *The Wiz* [1978] as the Scarecrow) was to play the lead, but Spielberg has insisted all along that the rumor was untrue (he blames the media for starting the rumor and fueling it). What is true about *Peter Pan* is that Spielberg plans to cast a young boy (not a female as in the Disney version) in the part.

After *Peter Pan* is completed, Spielberg plans to direct the third installment of Indiana Jones's adventures, currently in the planning stages at Lucasfilm.

Spielberg's plan for a "musical" with Quincy Jones, mentioned in a 1982 interview, was thought to be *The Color Purple* project. In actuality, Quincy Jones was contractually tied to *The Color Purple* when Warner Brothers offered it to Spielberg several years ago. Spielberg asserts that there are still plans to develop a musical with Jones.

Plans for an animated film with cartoon animator Don Bluth, also mentioned by Spielberg in a 1982 interview, will be released sometime in 1986; Spielberg also stated that he has lined up three such animated projects with Bluth, each project taking about three years to complete.

Rental Information

Most of the major film studios and distributors, such as Universal, United Artists, Paramount and others, have 16-mm rental divisions, but these rentals are often expensive and the film requested may not be currently available or even in distribution. Other sources, such as Audio-Brandon or Budget Films, Inc., are usually less expensive in the event the film is available from them.

The reader should be advised that most of Steven Spielberg's work is on videotape and can be locally rented at a fraction of the cost of a 16-mm film rental (usually under $5.00), or it may be purchased directly from a local video supplier. The purchase prices for Spielberg's films on videotape range from approximately $39.95 for *Raiders of the Lost Ark* to $89.95 for *Close Encounters of the Third Kind* (the most popular version of *Close Encounters* currently on tape is the special edition). Films that are not currently available as of this writing are *I Wanna Hold Your Hand* (1978), *E.T.: The Extra-Terrestrial* (1982), *The Color Purple* (1985) and Spielberg's 1985 releases as executive producer, *The Goonies,* and *Back to the Future,* and *Young Sherlock Holmes.*

Index